U T E
Legends

Celinda Reynolds Kaelin

illustrations by Manuel Pulido

Caxton Press

For my friend, my teacher,
Sowah Nanaen, Clifford Duncan
And for my dear sister,
Tatanka Win, Loya Colorow Arrum

Caxton Press

Library of Congress Cataloging-in-Publication Data

Names: Kaelin, Celinda Reynolds, author.
Title: Ute Legends / Celinda Reynolds Kaelin.
Description: Caldwell, Idaho : Caxton Press, 2017. | Includes
  bibliographical references and index.
Identifiers: LCCN 2017011174 | ISBN 9780870046056 (alk. paper)
Subjects: LCSH: Ute Indians--Folklore. | Ute mythology.
Classification: LCC E99.U8 K34 2017 | DDC 979.004/974576--dc23
  LC record available at https://lccn.loc.gov/2017011174

Cover and book design by Jocelyn Robertson

Printed and bound in the United States of America

CAXTON PRESS
Caldwell, Idaho
195015

U T E
Legends

Table of Contents

Foreword

It is not often that Non-Indian people are compelled to study, research, and document a true and accurate depiction of the lore of the native people that once occupied their homelands. And often, when it is entertained, it does not always reflect depth and quality content required because it does not have the commitment, sincerity, and spirit required to make it powerful and inspiring. Celinda Reynolds Kaelin, *Sunif Mamuch*, grew up with a deep appreciation for the past and present culture of her beloved Colorado. She was inspired not only by the classical Spanish-American influence of western culture but by its ancient past as well.

For most of her younger years and the past 20 years in particular, Kaelin dedicated her life to learning about the Ute people, especially the band of the Utes who lived in the area known as Tabeguache, today referred to as Uncompaghre. As with most areas throughout the U.S., the recorded history of the native people is often inaccurate, if told at all. Recognizing this limitation, Kaelin not only studied and continues to learn more about the Ute history, but also she has delved deeply into the meaning, messages, and interpretation of ancient legends and lore. As a result, Kaelin has acquired a deep and abiding understanding of Ute culture. For instance, as with many native tribes, the Ute close connection to nature is reflected in its animal tales. Also, since the Ute did not have a written culture, it is understood that an oral culture requires heightened accuracy in storytelling.

These and many more nuances make Kaelin's work valuable and a great contribution to understanding native peoples.

Ute Legends is a masterful work that recognizes and honors the lore of the Ute Indian people, a branch of the Shoshone Nation who, upon acquiring the horse, expanded their territory to include most of the two state areas of Colorado and Utah. Two of the predominant bands of Ute who occupied the lands in Kaelin's work were the Tabeguache and Yamparika. Both Ute bands, now referred to as Uncompaghre and White River respectively, were removed to the state of Utah in 1881 in response to the Meeker Massacre of 1879.

In Ute Legends, Kaelin has painstakingly compiled colorful tales of frogs, eagles, wolves, and other animals told in an authentic, engaging, and compelling style-usually with a keen sense of humor and often with a moral. Why were the Ute so emphatic that these stories be retold in exactly the same way from generation to generation? Is it because they contained vital information, such as how to start a fire or what actually happened at the end of the last Ice Age? These and many other questions are inspired by this work.

Celinda Reynolds Kaelin, *Sunif Mamuch*, is an adopted member of the Northern Ute Nation. She worked as assistant to Northern Ute Medicine Man, *Sowah Nanaen*, for over twenty years. Together they traveled and performed sacred ceremony in the Pikes Peak region and throughout North, Central, and South America with the World Council of Elders. She carries the Sacred Pipe, and has participated in the sacred Sun Dance with her Ute sisters *Tatanka Win* (the late Loya Arrum) and *Wankinyan Iktomi Win* (Kerry Cesspooch) for fifteen years. She resides with her husband, Harold, on a ranch in Tabeguache Ute territory near Tava (Pikes Peak).

I recommend this book for readers of all ages, from native studies scholars to the average native adult and especially children.

Forrest S. Cuch, Ute
Former Executive Director, Utah Division of Indian Affairs
Editor, A *History of Utah's American Indians* (Utah Division of Indian Affairs, 2000)
Utah, 2015

Acknowledgments

I am extremely grateful to the Ute Nation for the great care they have taken in preserving their legends. Almost all of the stories in this volume are from the Northern Ute who were emphatic that they be passed down through the generations verbatim. But why? This caution is what captured my attention as to their importance.

In working with Clifford Duncan (the Northern Ute Spiritual Leader and cultural liaison) we would spend weeks and even months recording, transcribing, and editing until the legends were correct. Again, I asked myself "Why is such great care taken with these stories?" After years of work, the legends that Clifford and I had worked so hard on were ready to go into a book. However, the Ute elders refused their permission, insisting that they remain an oral tradition. Years later, they changed their mind, but we had no time to pursue the project together again. However, I collected other Ute legends through my independent research over the last twenty years. This book is the result.

I can never thank Clifford enough for all that he taught me, but take some comfort from knowing that in the Spirit World he will know how grateful I am. I feel that he and my Ute sister Loya guided and supported this work for their Nation.

Manuel Pulido brings a deeper understanding of these stories with his charming illustrations. He is an incredibly gifted artist, and brings rich insights from his Apache culture. This seems a fitting collaboration, as the Jicarilla Apache were one of the few allies of the Ute Nation. I so enjoyed working with him, and was honored to have such a talented artist involved in the project.

Melinda Slawson, my daughter, my husband Harold, and my dear friend Stephanie DiCenzo were invaluable in helping me to catch all of my typos and grammatical errors. Any that slipped through are strictly from my oversight. I am deeply indebted to the researchers and authors whose work enlightened my understanding of the historical and cultural aspects of the legends, and have listed their works in the bibliography.

Scott Gipson at Caxton Press is a special force in bringing this book to life, and is a delight to work with, as are my editors at Caxton. Finally, I would like to thank fellow author Forrest Cuch, a special friend of both Clifford and Loya, for his support and help.

Introduction

About twenty years ago, as I was researching my first book *Pikes Peak Backcountry* [Caxton, 1999], I was conquered by the Ute Nation. My father, the late John P. Reynolds, Sr., taught us as children that you could judge a man's character by the way he treated his animals. Therefore, when I found historic reports of Ute warriors bathing their horses in Colorado's hot springs, I was hooked. Their Euro-American contemporaries thought it barbaric that they took care of their animals and failed to use the mineral waters for themselves. However, I viewed this as the highest type of character endorsement.

Fortunately for me, the Northern Ute Nation assigned a cultural liaison, Clifford Duncan, to review my writings on their nation. We worked together over the phone and through the mail for about six months. One day in late fall, I picked up the phone to Clifford's resonating, whispery voice, informing me that he was coming to meet me face to face. That same evening, six massive bull elk began frequenting our barn yard. They grazed on the leftover hay, and then bedded down on the stray wisps latticing the perimeter of the corrals. Each morning, they contentedly chewed their cuds while my husband Harold went about his chores. This unusual behavior continued for over three weeks. Finally, Clifford arrived late one afternoon.

As we shook hands, I noted that he towered a hand's width above Harold's five foot nine inches. When he removed his beaded ball cap, I noted his high, intelligent forehead and two long, traditional braids that trailed down his back. We then sat at the kitchen table, getting acquainted over a cup of coffee. He shared that his mother was a Medicine Woman and his father a Medicine Man, and also his grandmother and grandfather. (Clifford prefers the term "Spiritual Interpreter.") I knew this Medicine tradition was passed from one generation to the next, so I ran upstairs and got some tobacco, presenting it to Clifford as Medicine Man. He began telling me about his work, specifically about his Spirit Helpers from the animal world. It seems that Elk is his principal helper.

Early next morning, I gingerly sipped a steaming cup of coffee while gazing across the pasture as the coming sun splashed haphazard streaks of coral behind Pikes Peak. As if on cue, the six bull elk sauntered up to the corral, and then meandered down the pasture in front of the kitchen window.

"Clifford, come and see your helpers!"

Harold handed the Medicine Man a mug of coffee, as he came to stand by my side at the window. As soon as we were standing together, the elk also arranged themselves side by side in a military-style formation, and began to walk straight toward us. When they reached the fence (about twenty feet away), they raised their heads in unison and looked straight at us. Goose bumps covered my entire body as their trophy antlers, golden from the rising sun, pierced the pomegranate sky.

"Look Clifford, your helpers are saluting you!"

"No," he said, "the Elk People are telling me about us. We must work together." Not understanding the weight of the situation, I replied "Oh, thank you so much, but I am very busy right now."

"No," he said emphatically, "we must work together NOW!"

*

The next step of my journey began several weeks later.

"I must go to that place with the large, red rocks." Clifford informed me on one of his now periodic visits.

"You mean the Garden of the Gods?"

"Yes, that's the place. These are the bones of our Grandfathers, and I must bathe all of my ceremonial items in their dust."

We passed the hour drive from the ranch in contemplative silence until the cerise Grandfathers' Bones peered above the rooftops on our left.

Clifford abruptly broke the silence. "Do you have an Indian name?"

"No. It really never occurred to me to look for one."

"You must have one for your work. So, now you are Wolf Woman. *Sunif Mamuch* in our language. Wolf is your helper. When you need to call him, you must sing this song:"

BayKay (welcome) Su-Knife (Sunawiv, wolf)
Hey Yah Hey Yo Hay
BayKay Su-Knife
Hey Yah Hey Yo Hay
BayKay Su-Knife
Hey Yah Hey Yo Hay
BayKay Su-Knife
Hey Yah Hey Yo Hay

BayKay BayKay
Su-Knife Su-Knife

BayKay Su-Knife
BayKay Su-Knife
BayKay Su-Knife
BayKay Su-Knife
Hey Yah Hooooooooo

"These songs are like Spirits just floating around, and all you have to do is reach out and catch one. I caught this one for you."

*

In the many years that have passed since my naming, I have grown to love the Ute people as my own. I worked as Clifford's assistant in the World Council of Elders, and he performed ceremony to adopt me as Ute. I was adopted as "sister" by two very dear Ute women, Loya Arrum and Kerry Cesspooch. Together, we have Sun Danced for fifteen years. Sadly, both Clifford and Loya made their Journey to the Spirit World in 2014. Through my work with them, however, I inherited a wonderful extended Ute family.

In the Ute Agreement of 1880, the Northern Ute people were dispossessed of their ancestral lands in Colorado and forcibly removed to a reservation in Utah. This included the Ute band at *Tava*, Pikes Peak. The Pikes Peak Historical Society has established an endowment fund to bring the *Tabeguache* (People of Tava) back to their sacred mountain each year. This week of ceremony and visiting is always bittersweet, as the people are so emotionally attached to this land of their ancestors.

All that I can do is try to build bridges of understanding between our cultures. Toward this end, so that my speaking is informed, I have studied Ute history and collected dozens of their legends . I am constantly amazed at the power of these stories. Even first and second graders can repeat them almost verbatim after just one telling. In the traditional Ute way, these stories were only told in the winter by someone called *tu-gwe-wa-gunt*[1] (storyteller). Powell relates his particular

[1]   Catherine S. and Don D. Fowler, *Anthropology of the Numa: John Wesley Powell's Manuscripts on the Numic Peoples of Western North America, 1868-1880* (Smithsonian Institution Press, 1971) 21.

experience with one storyteller.

> Having finished our business for the evening, I asked
> if there was a "tu-gwe-wa-gunt" in camp – that is, if
> there was anyone present who was skilled in relating
> their mythology. Chuar said that To-mor-ro-un-ti-kai,
> the chief of these Indians, the Uinkarets, was a very
> noted man for his skill in this matter; but they both
> objected, by saying that the season [winter time] for
> tu-gwe-nai had not yet arrived. But I had anticipated
> this, and soon some members of the party came with
> pipes and tobacco, a large kettle of coffee, and tray of
> biscuits, and after sundry ceremonies of pipe-lighting
> and smoking, we all feasted; and, warmed up by this
> (to them unusual) good living, it was decided that the
> night should be spent in relating mythology.[2]

Unfortunately, Powell did not understand Ute
cosmology when he interpreted these stories. It is
quite different than our society's Judeo-Christian
concept of a male deity, up above the earth somewhere,
presiding over "heaven." For the Ute, the Supreme
Being, the Creator, is everywhere and within everything.
Creator is truly omnipresent. Therefore, Creator can
communicate with two-leggeds (human beings) through
a cloud, an eagle, a tree, a stone, a wolf, etc. Powell
misunderstood, however, and thought that this method
of communicating with the natural world indicated a
"savage stage of cultural evolution." The Fowlers go on
to suggest that the, "Numic tales that Powell gathered
were all 'zootheistic' in his terms and thus confirmed
the status of the 'Numa' [Ute] as 'savages.'"[3] How sad that
this opportunity for understanding between our cultures
was lost in the course of Powell's ethnographic work.

---

2   Fowler, *Anthropology of the Numa* 21.
3   Fowler, 21.

If he had understood the full import of unitheisism (an omnipresent Creator), it might have changed the way our cultures interacted.

These myths and legends can also make a significant contribution to our knowledge of Ute pre-history and culture. Oral tradition is too often dismissed without understanding its underlying integrity among indigenous people. Cushing observed this first hand when he lived among the Zuni.

"If you are told that any primitive people is ignorant of its history, don't believe it," said he [Cushing]. "They know all about it." And he told with what wonderful accuracy traditions are handed down among the Zunis, the tales, repeated thousands of times, being transmitted from father to son without the change of a single word, for generation after generation.[4]

My first clue to the validity of Cushing's observation on the link between legend and history came while researching the pre-history of the Ute people. Many historians have speculated about the genesis of the Uto-Aztecan culture and its connections to Mesoamerica, and I was intrigued by the possibilities this raised. Therefore, I delved into a study of Central and South American history and culture. While studying the Mayan codices, I experienced an epiphany of sorts when I found the glyph of a grumpy Rabbit who had just killed the sun with his club – this was the same story given in Ute legend over a thousand years later! I wondered how many other Ute legends could be linked to Mesoamerica.

To explore these origins, however, I felt that I had to first find the common threads of the many variations of the stories. I felt that once a uniform basis

---

4   Frank Hamilton Cushing, *My Adventures in Zuni* (Filter Press, 1998) 64.

was established, it would be easier to trace each legend's origins. In the footnotes at the beginning of each chapter you will notice that most of the legends have at least two or three variations. I trimmed these variables away to find their common core and was surprised to see how closely the tales then resembled the stories as told by my Northern Ute informants. I then added dialog, action, and background. Unfortunately, when ethnographers recorded the legends they tended to capture only the narrative facts. This approach relegates the tales to mere recitation of information and captures none of their vibrancy and charm. My children and grandchildren have taught me the importance of telling stories charged with drama. I still remember their delighted giggles when I changed my voice for each character, as grandparents of all cultures have been similarly taught. Ute *tu-gwe-wa-gunt* employed this same technique, and it was this dialog that gave life to the legends and imprinted them in the memories of generations.

I felt compelled to write this book so that the full impact of these stories could be experienced. In the pages that follow I have taken the legends from the fieldwork of ethnographers and infused them with the life of voice and dialog. The legends in Chapters 2, 3, 16, and 20 are informed by Smith's *Ute Tales*. However, they are also influenced by my Ute informants' telling of them, and I have charged the dialog I created with these cultural nuances. I have found that standing beside my Ute relatives, doing ceremony, opens a completely different type of dialog than an ethnographer might experience. The legends in Chapter 1, 4, 5, 9, 10, 11, 13, 14, and 15 are from Powell's fieldwork among the Northern Utes. These are also deeply influenced by my Ute informants. These same informants are the sole source of the legends in Chapter 6, 12, and 18.

Finally, the tribe compiled their own ethnographic

work in a small volume of legends, *Stories of Our Ancestors*, but again in narrative format. The stories in Chapter 7, 8, 17, and 19 are derived from this book but informed by Powell's and Smith's ethnographic work. This editing and blending of the different sources is used in virtually all the stories so that I could find their common core and perhaps link it to an ancient cultural source.

When I asked Clifford why he named me *Sunif Mamuch*, he explained that Wolf represents communication. When Wolf was near, the people knew that herds of buffalo, deer, or elk were also near. When Wolf howled, people knew that an enemy or a stranger was approaching. Wolf meant life for the people, and that is why Great Spirit adopted the form of Wolf whenever He/She took on a physical shape. As writer, speaker, teacher, and as friend, Clifford taught me to let Great Spirit flow through me and guide my work. This is Wolf medicine.

Therefore, I offer this collection of legends in order to expand and clarify our knowledge of the pre-history of the Ute people, including their origins and cultural affiliations. It will surprise many to see unmistakable links to the Anasazi and to the Toltec/Maya.

What follows in these pages are some of my favorite Ute tales. I hope that you will appreciate them in the light of Ute cosmology. These are clearly a people with a deep love for the natural world and who have an incredibly rich culture and pre-history. I will forever be thankful that Clifford listened to the Elk People.

The One-Two Boys, So-Kus Wai-Un-Ats [5]

Tum-pwi-nai-ro-gwi-nump (He Who Had a Stone Shirt) killed *Sikor* (Crane) and stole his wife. As they were about to embark on the journey to his land, he scolded his new woman.

"You cannot bring your child with you! We must travel quickly before Crane's people come after us. You must kill that little one, now!"

"Very well, but I must gather my things for our journey." And with that the mother turned her back on Stone Shirt and hid the baby under her dress. She slipped into her lodge, and then out the back and hurried to the child's grandmother, where she left him.

Years passed, and the little boy grew healthy and strong. He was a joy to his grandmother, and she cherished his company wherever she went. One day, they were digging roots near the river. This was usually hard work, but today the boy only gave a gentle tug and the roots flew out of the earth.

"Grandmother, see how easily the roots come out of Mother Earth! Why is this?"

"I do not know, Grandson. We have much work to do, so let us continue."

Now, the roots simply fell into their hands when they touched them, and they both looked in awe at one another. Grandmother shook her head in wonderment.

5 Fowler, *Anthropology of the Numa* 82-85.

"Aieeeee! Surely some strange thing is about to happen, Grandson."

The boy ran over to the pile of roots they had dug and found many missing.

"Grandmother, did you take the roots away?"

"No, my child, perhaps some ghost has carried them off. Let us dig no more. Come away!"

But the boy was too curious. "I will find what all this means," he said to himself, and began to search the entire area. At last he came upon a man sitting under a tree and angrily confronted him.

"You are a thief! What did you steal, our roots? That is all that my Grandmother and I have to eat!" And with that he began to throw mud and stones at the man until he broke the stranger's leg. Still the stranger said nothing, but remained silent and sorrowful. He slowly rose, tied his broken leg with sticks, bathed it in the river, and then sat down under the tree again. He waived his arm at the boy, inviting him to come near.

"My son," he began gently, "I have something very important to tell you. Did that old woman ever tell you about your mother and father?"

"No," answered the boy, "I have never heard of them."

"My son, do you see these bones scattered on the ground? Whose bones are these?"

"How should I know," said the boy, "it may be that some elk or deer has been killed here."

"No," answered the man.

"Well, perhaps they are the bones of a bear."

But the man just shook his head. The boy continued naming other animals, but the man only frowned and continued to shake his head.

"These are the bones of your father. Stone Shirt killed him and left him to rot here on the ground like a wolf."

Clinching his jaw, the boy now looked in anger at what had been done to his father. Now the stranger asked him another question.

"Is your mother in the lodge over there?"

"No."

"Does your mother live on the banks of this river?"

Looking down at his feet, the boy sadly shook his head and replied, "I don't know my mother, I have never seen her. She is dead."

"My son," replied the stranger, "Stone Shirt, who killed your father, stole your mother and took her away to the shore of a distant lake and there she is his wife today."

At this, the boy turned away from the man and wept bitterly. When he turned around again, the stranger had disappeared. He wiped his tears and felt the anger rising up in his heart against this man who had killed his father and stole his mother. He hurried to his grandmother's lodge where he confronted her.

"Grandmother, why have you lied to me about my father and mother?"

She could not bear the angry and disappointed look in the boy's eyes, so she bowed her head, knowing that a spirit had told him the truth. Her grandson fell to the ground, weeping bitterly until he fell into a deep sleep. He slept for three days and three nights.

When he finally awoke, he told his grandmother, "I am going out to gather all the nations to help me in my fight."

The boy traveled throughout the land, telling his story and asking for help in avenging his father's death. Finally, he returned with many nations, including *Shin-au-av* (Wolf) and *To-go-av* (Rattlesnake). Grandmother fed all three, and when they had filled their bellies, the boy walked over to her.

"Grandmother, cut me in two!" he demanded.

"Grandson, you ask me something that I cannot do.

I love you too dearly."

"Cut me in two!" he again demanded, and handed her a stone ax that he had brought from a far away country. She saw the determined look on his face, and reluctantly took the ax from his hands. Slowly she raised it over her head, and closing her eyes she brought its blade down on the boy with all her strength. When she opened her eyes she was horrified to see that she had, indeed, cut the boy in two, so she fled in terror. Within moments, however, each of the two parts of the beautiful boy became a complete man, each so similar to the other that no one could tell them apart.

Wolf and Rattlesnake lost no time in going throughout the village of all nations, telling them of this wonderful thing that had happened to the boy.

"It is a powerful thing that has happened. What was one is now two. You can see for yourselves that there are now two boys instead of one! They are So-kus Wai-un-ats (the One-Two Boys). Surely the Spirits are showing that we will be successful in our journey to kill Stone Shirt. We must avenge the death of the boy's father!"

As they began their journey, the One-Two Boys carried between them a magical cup filled with water. Earlier, while the boy slept for three days, he had been told in a dream about this cup. Therefore, he searched for it on his journey among the nations and brought it back with him. Now he and his brother carried it between them as they led the nations on their journey. On their left walked Rattlesnake and on their right walked Wolf, and all the other nations followed behind them in the order that they had been contacted.

After many miles of travel the people began to tire and grew thirsty. They could find no water, however, and fell onto the sand groaning and complaining.

"These One-Two Boys have deceived us! We will all die on this journey!"

Fortunately, the One-Two Boys had been warned of this in their wonderful dream. They knew that the people would suffer, but that the water that they carried in the magical cup was only to be used as a last resort. The boys looked at one another and said, "Now the time has come for us to drink the water." Lifting the cup to his lips, the first brother tilted his head back and drained it. Incredibly, the cup filled with water again and so the second brother drank it all but it still refilled itself. The two boys passed among the people, giving them water from the cup, and no matter how many times it was passed, it continued to be filled to the brim with water.

In the meantime, however, Wolf lay dead from thirst on the ground. The people mourned him deeply because he was a great man. The boys heard their wails of sorrow and held the cup over Wolf, sprinkling him with its water. He slowly began to move, jumped to his feet, and demanded, "Why do you disturb me? I was having a vision of mountain streams and meadows and wonderful things to eat!" The boys handed him the cup and Wolf threw his head back, drinking all the water. This time the cup did not refill itself. All of the people were now refreshed, and their spirits were high, so they continued their journey.

By the middle of the next day, however, the people were weak with hunger. Again, they complained, "These One-Two Boys have deceived us! We will all die on this journey!" The boys heard their angry voices but when they looked up at the ridge line ahead of them they saw an antelope standing boldly outlined against the sky.

Wolf knew that it was *Tau-shants* (Antelope With Many Eyes) who was the lookout for Stone Shirt.

"I will go and kill Many Eyes so that we may safely attack Stone Shirt," Wolf declared. Rattlesnake, however, had a different idea on how to proceed.

"It will be much better if I go and kill him, as he will certainly see you and run away."

"No, *To-go-av*," said the One-Two Boys. "*Shin-au-av* must go and kill *Tau-shants*. This is how it must be."

Wolf set off at a lope, ranging in a wide arc to the left of antelope. He planned to circle around some low hills and come upon him from the other side. Meanwhile, Rattlesnake went a little way from the camp, calling back to the brothers.

"Do you see me now?"

They looked all around the nearby hills but could not see him.

"Hunt for me!" Rattlesnake called to them, and they began to look under every bush and rock. He taunted them, saying, "I can see you! You are looking under that big boulder. Now you are looking under the rabbit bush. Can't you see me?" Still they could not find him. "Now you know that I can see others and that I cannot be seen when I so desire. *Shin-au-av* cannot kill that antelope for he has many eyes and is the wonderful watchman of Stone Shirt, but I can kill him for I can go to where he is and he cannot see me."

At last the boys were convinced.

"You go then, *To-go-av*. Kill *Tau-shants*. Then we may have our revenge on Stone Shirt."

When Wolf saw that Rattlesnake had killed Antelope, he was angry.

"I am a great hunter! It was my right to kill *Tau-shants*, not *To-go-av's*." He charged up the hill intent on killing his rival. When he came near to Antelope, however, he saw that he was nice and fat, and that he would make a rich feast for the people. He sighed deeply and said to himself, "What does it matter who kills the game when we can all eat it?" The people ate until their bellies were full and then the resumed their journey.

The next day the people again complained of being very thirsty. The One-Two Boys had been told in a dream what to do, for the magical cup was empty, so they turned

24

themselves into doves and flew away. At last they came to a lake near the home of Stone Shirt. They circled above the lake, coming closer and closer to the ground where they saw two beautiful maidens bathing in the water. They flew into some bushes nearby so that they could get a better look at the girls, but were soon caught in a snare the girls had placed there. The beautiful maidens came up and took the birds out of the snare. They held them gently in their hands and examined them.

"I have never seen such interesting birds! They are wonderful! Let us take them home to show Father." They carried the birds home and showed them to Stone Shirt.

"My daughters," he said, "I very much fear that these are spies from my enemies, for such birds do not live in our land. I must destroy them!" He was about to throw them into the fire when the girls cried and grabbed his legs.

"Father, please, we beg of you! Don't kill them! They are the most beautiful birds we have ever seen. Let us take them back to the lake and set them free."

Stone Shirt could not deny his daughters, even though his heart told him that this was the wrong thing to do. As soon as the birds were free they flitted among the bushes along the shore until they found the magical cup. They carried it to the middle of the lake and gently settled in the water with it. The maidens saw all this and supposed that they had drowned. However, once the cup was filled with water, the birds lifted it and carried it back to their people in the desert. They were just in time, and just as before, each person drank from the cup and it magically filled itself again and again. When everyone finally had enough, there was not a drop left in the cup. The brothers then told the people that they had seen Stone Shirt and his daughters.

The next day they all arrived near the home of Stone Shirt. The brothers were now back in their human form and they went to scout their enemy. As they came near, they found a woman gathering seeds and recognized her as their mother whom Stone Shirt had stolen from Si-kor (Crane). The excited boys ran up to her.

"Mother, Mother, it is us! Your lost sons!"

She looked from one to the other and sadly shook her head. "No, this cannot be. I had only one son."

"Yes, that is us! When you left us with Grandmother, Spirit visited us and told us to have her split me in two with an ax. When she did that, each half of ourself became a full person! Now we are two! We have brought many people with us to avenge our father's death and take you home."

Weeping, she fiercely embraced her long-lost sons. "No, no! I beg of you. Stone Shirt is too powerful. No arrows can penetrate his armor. He is a great warrior and he delights in killing his enemies. Even his daughters have magical powers. They have bows and arrows that the can shoot so fast that they fill the air like a cloud. They don't even have to take aim! Their arrows go where they will them. All they have to do is to think the arrows into the hearts of their enemies. These girls can kill all of your people before a common person can even shoot one arrow."

"Mother, we will be okay. Do not be afraid. We were shown in our dream that *Tum-pwi-nai-ro-gwi-nump* will be killed. We will attack at dawn tomorrow, so you must leave his house and go down to the lake where you will be safe."

During the night, the One-Two Boys transformed themselves into mice, and then scampered to the home of Stone Shirt. They found the magical bows and arrows of his daughters. With their sharp teeth, they gnawed on the sinew on the backs of the bows and then nibbled the bow-strings so that they were worthless. Rattlesnake had followed them and hid under a rock near by.

26

At dawn the next morning, Stone Shirt rose from his buffalo robes and went out of his tipi to greet the sun. He yawned and stretched, feeling strong and safe, and then sat on a nearby rock. Rattlesnake, coiled underneath, sprang at his enemy and sank his fangs into Stone Shirt's leg. He bellowed in pain and jumped into the air.

"Daughters! Daughters! We are betrayed! The enemy is here! Attack, attack!"

The girls grabbed their bows and arrows and dashed out of the lodge to defend their father. However, when they placed the arrows on their bow strings they crumbled in their hands. Now all of the people rushed forward to attack but the girls waved them back and indicated that they would parley. They slowly approached the body of their dead father then sadly stood over him and sang their Death Song. They then began to whirl in giddy circles, faster and faster, dancing their Death Dance. Finally, exhausted, they fell to the ground dead.

The warrior twins buried the maidens near the shore of the lake. However, they left the body of Stone Shirt to rot. His bones were left to bleach on the sands just as he had left Crane's.

WHAT CAN WE LEARN FROM "THE ONE-TWO BOYS"?

This legend is illuminating on two levels.

First, it teaches the quality of endurance. Powell clarified this point in his notes on the legend, saying that there is a proverb among the Utes: "Do not murmur when you suffer in doing what the spirits have commanded for a cup of water is provided." He adds that the Utes attach a second proverb to this story: "What matters who kills the game when we can all eat of it?"

The second interesting aspect of this story is the insights it gives us as to the origins of the Ute Nation. In a discussion on the ancestral lands of the Anasazi, Madsen writes that "the region was historically occupied by the Utes and Southern Paiutes and either there has been an expansion of Numic [Uto-Aztecan] speakers into the area during the last 500-1000 years or the *Anasazi of Mesa Verde are the ancestors of the Ute*."[6] [emphasis added]

Among archaeologists, the Warrior-Hero Twin myths are used as a cultural marker for the descendants of the Anasazi – the Hopi and the Puebloans. Now we can add the Ute people as Anasazi progeny based on their myth of the Warrior-Hero Twins. If this link is valid in establishing the Hopi and the Pueblo Peoples as descendants of the Anasazi, then the Ute People must be added as well.

In Hopi tradition, the Creator is *Tawa*, the Sun Spirit. (This is similar to the Ute, but their word is *Tava*.) *Tawa* created *Sotuknang*, who then created Spider Grandmother who created the Sacred Twins, *Poqanghoy* and *Palongawhoya*.[7]

---

6 David B Madsen and David Rhode, editors, *Across the West: Human Population Movement and the Expansion of the Numa* (Utah UP, 1994) 24.

7 Frank Waters and Oswals White Bear Fredericks, *The Book of the Hopi* (Viking Penguin Books, 1963) 3.

It seems only logical, therefore, that the existence of the Sacred Twin myth in Ute culture gives them entrée to this Anasazi cultural fraternity. This argument is predicated, of course, on the fact that all of these peoples are part of the Uto-Aztecan language group, and that they also share a common homeland. This brings us to another interesting point: linking these peoples to Mesoamerica.

The sacred book of the Maya, "*The Popol Vuh*," presents what is probably the earliest legend of the hero twins. This Quiche Maya story was recorded from the original bark document around 1554, and then translated to Spanish in 1700. The Mayan twins also have a miraculous birth, live with their grandmother, and overcome a supernatural enemy to secure a future for their people.

The Hopi, Puebloan, and Ute hero twin stories share these common elements. They have a miraculous birth, live with their grandmother, enlist all of the animal nations in their quest, overcome a supernatural enemy, and are the progenitors of their people. These legends are just one facet in documenting the connections of these Uto-Aztecan people (Ute, Hopi, Anasazi) and Toltec-Maya. However, and perhaps more importantly, we have the language itself.

Noted archaeologist, Stephen Lekson, emphasizes this linguistic link between Ute and Hopi.

Piman is part of the larger Uto-Aztecan language family that includes Nahuatl, the Aztec language. In the southwest, Uto-Aztecan dominates west of [Highway] 666, with Ute and Hopi branches to the north and Piman to the south. This is a fact of fundamental importance to the history of the ancient Southwest. Mark it well.

Linguist David B. Madsen weighs in on the vital issue of a common language as well.

> The scanty language differentiation among Numic speakers in the Great Basin and around its peripheries, I hypothesize, resulted from the relative recency of the occupation of those areas by people who resided there at <u>Contact</u>. The expansion eastward (northeast and southeast, too) through the Great Basin and into its peripheries probably *did not begin much more than 2,000 years ago.*[8] [emphasis added]

There are yet two more important clues to Ute prehistory in this legend: Stone Shirt and the Crane People.

Aztec warriors used a type of body armor made of seven or eight thicknesses of deer skin. This leather jacket, or "stone" shirt, provided protection against arrows. This body armor was later adopted by the Spanish army as a *cueras* worn by the *Soldado de Cuera*, Leather Jacket Soldiers.[9]

In this legend, Stone Shirt steals the wife of Crane. Mexico has over 15 of the world's 63 species of heron. Among native peoples it is common to lump all of one species under a common name, such as "heron," rather than use the word crane. Therefore, "Stone Shirt" and "Crane" give us another possible link to the Aztec. Aztec historian, Rick Holmer, gives us further clarification.

> The people we call Aztecs did not refer to themselves by that name but called themselves Mexica

8   Madsen, *Across the West* 85
9   San Diego History Journal, 73 Winter. Also, "Making Sense of the Leather Jackets (Cueras) worn in Northern New Spain." Jack S. Williams. The Center for Spanish Colonial Research, CA. 2001. 44.

from which we derive the name for the modern country of Mexico (which means 'the place of the Mexica"). Nineteenth century scholars, specifically Alexander van Humboldt and William Prescott, popularized the term Aztec, a shortened form of Azteca meaning "people from Aztlan". Aztlan, which means *"place of herons,"* was the original homeland.[10] (emphasis added.)

As you can see from this discussion of the One-Two Boys, Sacred Twins, this legend provides so much more than mere entertainment. It gives practical advice to the People regarding survival but, perhaps more importantly, it also provides invaluable clues as to the very origins of the Ute People.

---

10   Rick Holmer, *The Aztec Book of Destiny* (Book Surge, 2005) viii.

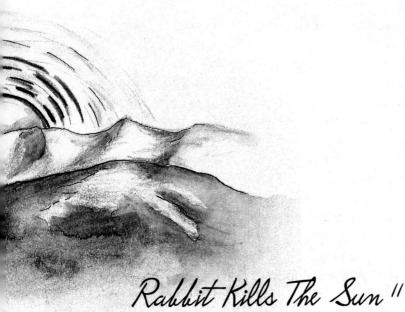

Rabbit Kills The Sun [11]

Along time ago, the sun was very, very hot. Much hotter than it is today. It was so hot that nothing could grow. Rabbit saw his people suffer because of this.

"I am going off to the place where the sun rises," he told his family. "And I am going to do something about it."

Rabbit set off early the next morning, carrying a large club, his *pogamoggan*, over his shoulder.

Now, Rabbit had two names. His first, or ordinary name, was *Tavooch*. But his second name, *Tav-weatch*, was sacred. Rabbit became angry if anyone called him by his ordinary name. He only liked his sacred name.

As Rabbit walked along, some weeds stood up and smiled.

"Good morning, *Tavooch*. Where are you going?"

Rabbit clinched his teeth and raised his club. *Bam!* Then *bam*, again. He smashed the weed until its green juices ran into the ground.

11   Uintah-Ouray Tribe, *Stories Of Our Ancestors* (Utah Printing Service UP 1974) 2. Anne M. Smith, *Ute Tales* (Utah UP, 1992) 23, 53-57.

"Why did you hit that man?" The other Weed People asked.

"Because he called me *Tavooch*."

As Rabbit ambled along to the top of the next mountain he saw yet another mountain range in the distance. Then he saw someone digging. It was *Quiagat* (Grizzly Bear).

"What are you doing?" asked Rabbit in his sweetest, most innocent voice.

"I am digging a hole so that I can hide from *Tavooch*. I heard that he is coming, and that he is mad and killing people. As soon as I see him coming, I am going to run and jump in my hole."

"Oh, that is a good idea," said Rabbit. "Show me how you are going to do this."

"This is how I am going to hide." And with that, Bear ran and jumped into his hole.

"How will you know when to jump into your hole?" asked Rabbit.

"Oh, when I hear *Tavooch* coming I will run and jump."

Rabbit asked him to show him his plan again. When he was in his hole, Rabbit asked, "Aren't you going to peek out to be sure that it is *Tavooch*?"

"Yes, I will look out like this."

And when Bear raised his head to look, *bam*, Rabbit hit and killed him. Hefting his club onto his shoulder, he continued his journey.

As he was climbing to the crest of the next mountain range, he heard children crying. Looking around, he saw two little winged ones.

"My children, why are you weeping?" asked *Tavooch*.

They wiped their tears with their feathers, and the bolder of the two replied.

"Good Morning, *Tavweatch*."

And Rabbit smiled at the use of his sacred name.

"We came out with our mother to gather Yampa, but as she was digging, a huge boulder rolled off the hillside and buried her. Now we are all alone," he whimpered.

"Well, what do you live on? How do you eat?" asked Rabbit.

"We are hungry! We eat whatever we can find."

"Have you any water?" continued Rabbit.

"No. Every time we go to the stream, it splashes all over us and then we are cold and wet."

Rabbit frowned and asked, "How do you keep warm at night?"

"We tried to gather firewood, but the tree blew sparks onto us and made blisters."

Rabbit pounded his club on the ground. "Close your eyes and turn around. Don't look!"

Ruffling their feathers, the little boys turned their backs to Rabbit and closed their eyes.

Bam! Bam! Rabbit struck the tree a severe blow.

"Now," he declared "even old women and little children will be able to gather your branches for fire."

He raised his club again, and this time attacked the stream. *Bam! Bam!*

"Now, even old women and children will be able to come to you when they need water."

"Grandsons, show me where the rock is that killed your mother."

Strutting over to the boulder, Rabbit set his club down and bent way over so that only his little tail was in the air. He pushed and shoved until the huge stone rolled off the Mourning Dove.

Rubbing her eyes, she yawned and stretched.

"Oh, what a nice sleep," she cooed. "I was gathering yampa when that rock fell on top of me." She then gathered her sons and the yampa and they all went home to eat.

Rabbit continued on his way until he came to *Tava*, Pikes Peak, the last mountain range and the place where the sun came up.

"Now how am I going to kill the Sun? He has eyes that see everywhere. When I am in one place, he sees me and then jumps to the other side. My people are suffering and I must kill him."

Someone was camped nearby, and he was singing. He stopped when he heard Rabbit talking to himself.

"Let me help you," said *Paa-caga-ci* (Spider). "I can make a web over your hole and Sun cannot see you."

Rabbit climbed into a hole and Spider spun his web.

When Sun began to climb into the sky the next morning, *bam, bam!* His eyes could not find Rabbit, but Rabbit's club found him!

Sun fell to the ground and everything was burning. Rabbit ran as fast as he could, just barely in front of the raging fire.

"Trees, Trees, save me! I killed Sun and set the world on fire!"

"We can't help you, as we will be only ashes."

"Stream, Stream, save me! I killed Sun and set the world on fire!"

"We can't help you, as soon we will be only steam."

Rabbit asked everyone for help, but no one could protect him. As he ran, he came to one little half-moon bush.

"Little Weed, can you help me?"

"Yes. Come! Hide under me. Fire will just go over me and make a noise."

Rabbit just had time to dig under Little Weed's branches when the fire roared past. Unfortunately, Little Weed didn't completely cover his long ears or his tail. That's why they are black to this day. Little Weed is called *Yu-a-nump*, Rabbit Bush, because he saved Rabbit's life that day.

Today, as people travel through the country side and see the black rocks, the lava, they say, "Oh, that is from the time that Rabbit killed the sun and set the world on fire."

WHAT CAN WE LEARN FROM "RABBIT KILLS THE SUN"?

This is one of my favorite legends to share with children. At first, I was reluctant to do so because of the violence. However, one day after watching an episode of Roadrunner and Coyote with my grandchildren, I realized that it was no more violent than most cartoons. Amazingly, I found that school children could almost remember the legend verbatim after one telling. I could only imagine being a Ute grandmother and telling it in the winter by the warmth of a tipi fire for four straight nights, and then asking each of the children in turn to repeat it. No wonder the oral tradition of the Ute is so strong. There is nothing better than a peer group of young people correcting your every word to ensure a legend's authenticity. This legend taught me something else quite amazing : the brilliance of this storytelling. These words are carefully chosen and the story carefully crafted for full impact. That is why their accuracy is so important, and why the *tu-gwe-wa-gunt* told the same *tu-gwe-nai*, legend, four times, and then required the students to repeat it verbatim.

"Rabbit Kills the Sun" is especially intriguing when you look at it as metaphor. Could it be an oral tradition documenting the Clovis Comet, an event from 13,000 years ago that killed off the Clovis people and caused the extinction of the Mammoths[12]?

Among many people of the Aztec language family, such as the Utes, Rabbit is a metaphor for the moon.[13] If you look carefully at the full moon you can see Rabbit's curved back along the left side, as his head and long ears arc over the top and to the right. Does Rabbit killing the

12   Proceedings of the National Academy of Sciences, 3/1/2012. Irene Klotz "New Clovis Comet Clues from Mexico, 3/14/2012.
13   Miguel Leon-Portilla, *Aztec Thought and Culture* (Oklahoma UP, 1963) 49-50.

sun indicate a full eclipse of the sun at some time in the past? Did an eclipse precede the arrival of the Clovis Comet? Are the fireballs from the comet actually the images used in the story of the sun falling to earth and setting it on fire?

This same story is told among the Maya. A detailed glyph from the late Classic Mayan Period (600 A.D.) shows rabbit holding a large club with which he has just killed an eagle, the Mayan symbol for the sun.[14] Among the Maya, Rabbit also symbolized the moon. In a version of this story as told to Powell in 1868, Rabbit survives by hiding in an ice cave.[15] Again, this is a plausible explanation for how the people survived the devastation of the Clovis Comet. Irene Klotz writes for New.Discovery.com.

> Geologists have unearthed new evidence that a massive asteroid or comet smashed into the planet, impacting nearly one-third of the earth, some 12,900 years ago ....during a period called the Younger Dryas, a time marked by unusual cold temperatures and the extinction of many large animals in North America, including mammoths, mastodons, and saber-tooth cats.[16]

This event had to have had a profound impact on the lives and the psyche of the indigenous people at that time. The Clovis culture completely disappeared and wasn't replaced until the Folsom people some 2,000 years later. It is no wonder then that this is one of the more enduring of Ute legends. It would also seem to corroborate origin stories of various indigenous people relating a re-emergence from the earth or from caves.

---

14   Mary Miller and Karl Taube, *The Gods and Symbols of Ancient Mexico and the Maya* (Thames and Hudson Ltd., 1993) 143.
15   Fowler, *Anthropology of the Numa* 246, 270.
16   Klotz.

The Dog Council [17]

A long time ago, the sun shone very hot and the rains did not come. There was no food in the land, and *Sarici* (the Dog People) were suffering.

They watched as the old ones went off to gather firewood. One day, Grandmother Dog wrapped her shawl closely around her shoulders and picked up the rope she used to bind the sticks together as she collected them in bundles. She slowly shuffled off through the snow, disappearing into the pine trees. When she was out of sight of the village, she sat down on a log and began to sing her death chant.

"Only the mountains and the sky live forever! Aiyeeeee."

Pitifully, she sang and sang until she grew so cold that her voice no longer worked. Then she fell into a deep sleep, and never returned to camp. She did not want to take precious food from the children.

One by one, the other Elders from the village also went off to gather wood. Even so, many of the children began to weaken and die.

The Chief sent runners to other villages and learned they suffered the same fate. He then had the runners return with a new message.

"Let us all come together in council and see what we can do to conquer this famine."

It was early *tamau'errawats*, and the sun's rays had not reached their full strength, so the snow lingered, sending tiny streams of water to mix with the red earth.

---

17   Smith, *Ute Tales* 39.

Still, the Dog People trudged through the mud for miles in order to reach the council tipi. The Chief had ordered his people to combine three large tipis into this one, large enough so that all of his guests could be seated around the council fire.

His guests were mindful of their good manners.

"Let us remove our leggings, for they are full of mud. We can hang them on this post." And one by one, they pulled off their soiled leggings and hung them on the post by the door.

Now the leggings of the Dog People are a little different than those for Two Leggeds. They run the entire length of their leg. However, their tails are also attached, and they made great, bushy bundles as they were piled on top of each other.

The Dog Chief loaded *Cuu-ci* (Peace Pipe) and passed it around to his guests.

"Now, my friends, we have smoked the sacred pipe so that we can talk about this terrible time of suffering."

Boom! No sooner were the words out of his mouth, than *tununiri* (Thunder), boomed and *tonapagari* (lightning), struck the tipi. Flames raced down the lodge poles!

"Ow, ow, ow!" Yelled the Dog People, and they all raced to get out of the tipi, hastily grabbing their leggings from the pole by the door. The terrified dogs ran and ran, disappearing into the woods in all directions.

But there was one lingering problem.

"Hey! These aren't my leggings!" echoed in every village. And to this day, each time one Dog Person meets another they immediately sniff under each other's tail.

"Have you got my leggings?"

And to this day every Dog Person carries that fear of Thunder.

WHAT CAN WE LEARN FROM "THE DOG COUNCIL"?

Among the Ute people, there was a special society of grandmothers and grandfathers who oversaw the breeding of their dogs and, later, horses. Members of this Twisted Hair Society were thought to possess special powers from the Creator for this work. They were easily identified by the distinctive knot of twisted hair on their forehead. Armed only with this signature hair style, they safely traveled from village to village among the First Nations, ensuring that only the most desirable animals reproduced.

This charming legend also provides insights on the use of the *Cuuci* (Sacred Pipe) by Utes. Ethnographer Ann Smith reports on the Pipe from her Ute informants.

> Colorado Utes described a custom where a group of young men would stand outside the tipi of a chief or leading man and sing, while beating on a piece of rawhide or a hand drum, until they were invited to enter, sit down and smoke. The pipe would be filled with tobacco by the host, lit with a long stick from the fire, then passed around clockwise...When all had smoked, the young men would move on to another tipi.[18]

Smith also gives a detailed description of the Ute Pipes.

> [These pipes were] made of red rock...The bowl was hollowed out with a large arrow point or spear point and the outside was rubbed with stone to smooth it... The stem was eight to fifteen inches long and was frequently made out of wild rose or of "kunu-kupi."... Leaves of wild tobacco, which grew plentifully on

---

18   Ann Smith, *Ethnography of the Northern Utes* (Museum of New Mexico Press, 1974) 118-120.

43

burned over areas, were gathered in the fall and dried in the sun. They were stored [after being mixed with lard, or kinnikinick] in a buckskin sack, and were rubbed between the hands before smoking.[19]

Poncha Springs and Poncha Pass in Colorado bear the Ute name for tobacco.

Clifford informed me that after the Native American Religious Crimes Act of 1883[20] was enacted, the Ute People took drastic measures to protect their sacred items.

The Ute People have a Sacred Pipe, but it is buried in a secret place. They buried their sacred things so that the soldiers would not take them. When the time is right, and animal will show the spot, and bring it up, and all people will be One.[21]

19   Smith, *Ethnography of the Northern Utes* 118-120.
20   Annual Report of the Secretary of the Interior [Senator Henry M. Teller], November 1, 1883.
21   Author interview, Clifford Duncan, 3/10/1998.

Origin of Echo [22]

It was now *ututatapi*, the golden autumn light, and *Iowi* (Mourning Dove) , busily gathered seeds in the valley. As the sun rose higher in the sky she began to tire, so she took the cradleboard from her back and gently set her baby under a large sagebrush.

"*Ohochu* (Yellow Bird) I must continue gathering food, so watch your little brother for me."

Obediently, the little yellow bird crouched on the ground near her brother, absently pecking at twigs here and there, trying to imitate her mother's work. As *Iowi* wandered further away, crafty *Tso-a-vwits* (Witch) carefully approached *Ohochu*.

"Is that your brother?" she asked in her sweetest, concerned voice.

Ohochu knew that witches always wanted to steal boys but wouldn't bother little girls, so she innocently replied, "No, this is my sister."

Tso-a-vwits frowned and gritted her teeth. "It is naughty for girls to lie!" And she put on a strange and horrid appearance. *Ohochu* froze in fear as she gazed at the hideous *Tso-a-vwits*, allowing the old woman to snatch the little boy and fly off to a distant mountain. When she landed, she laid the cradleboard on the ground, where she hastily unwrapped the baby from his blankets. She roughly grabbed his right foot and pulled and pulled until it stretched his leg to the length of a grown man's. She repeated the process with his left leg and then with each of his arms. When she finished her evil work the

---

22   Fowler, *Anthropology of the Numa* 263.

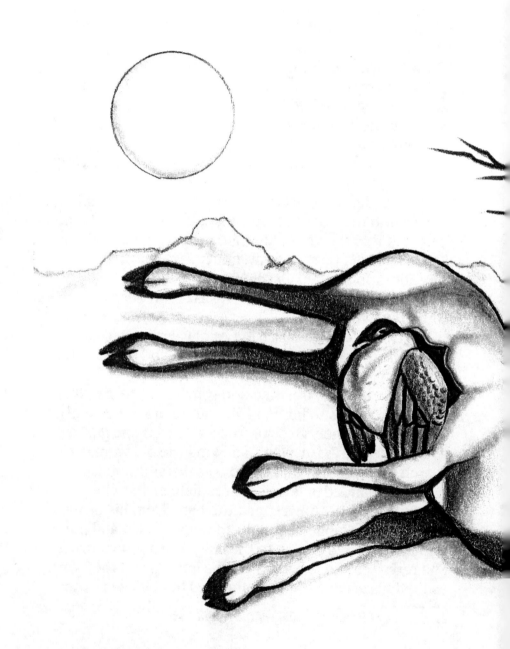

baby was as large as a man. "Now I have the husband that I have always wanted!" and she married him that same afternoon. Although *Uja* (the sage grouse) had the body of a man, he still had the heart of a baby and didn't know any better than to marry a witch. Meanwhile, his mother discovered his abduction.

"*Ohochu*, what have you done!" Mourning Dove raged at her daughter. "How could you let *Tso-a-vwits* take your brother?" The little yellow bird wept bitterly after the witch stole her brother, and even more so as her mother scolded her.

"My baby! My baby!" *Iowi* cried and cried, and could not be comforted. "I must have my baby back! I must! I must! Please, somebody, help me!" Eagle, her brother, heard her wailing and with a great whoosh of his wings, landed beside *Iowi*.

"Don't cry, little sister, I will find your baby and we will punish *Tso-a-vwits*."

"Oh, *Kwina*, you must hurry! I am afraid that something bad has happened to him. Hurry! Please hurry!" Whoosh, whoosh, *Kwina*'s great wings lifted him once again into the sky. He flew throughout the region, circling every valley and every mountain top. One day as he searched, he heard a strange noise. When he looked down he saw *Tso-a-vwits* and *Uja* but did not recognize his nephew in the body of this grown man. Puzzled, he returned to *Iowi* and told her what he had seen.

"If that is indeed my little boy, he will know me by my voice. Please show me where they are." So *Kwina* took Mourning Dove to the mountain where *Tso-a-vwits* lived with her husband. *Iowi* silently circled the spot and then landed in a cedar tree.

"Uja, *whoooo, whooo, whoo, whoo!*" She cried mournfully throughout the day and into the night as *Kwina* watched silently from a nearby tree.

"I hear my mother! I hear my mother!" Little Sage

Grouse jumped excitedly around his wife, but she only laughed at him.

"You foolish boy! It is a trick! You must hide quickly or a witch will grab you!" Tso-a-vwits quickly emptied the stomach of a mountain sheep they had just killed and both she and her husband climbed inside. "Surely Iowi will never look in the paunch of a mountain sheep for my husband and myself."

"Uja, whoooo, whooo, whooo, who!" Iowi closed her eyes as she continued to cry. When she finally opened them, the witch and her son were nowhere in sight. Kwina was also caught off guard. "Don't cry, Iowi, they are hidden somewhere. Maybe in the ground, or maybe under the rocks." He frowned and thought for a few more minutes before his eyes lit up. "Soon they will be hungry and will go to look for food. I will put something to eat in a tree and tempt them to come out of hiding." With a great whoosh, Eagle soared from his tree top and soon had a rabbit in his talons. He flew to the top of a large pine tree and laid the rabbit carcass in the branches. Then he peeled the bark from the bottom of the tree and trimmed all of the lower branches, making it difficult to climb.

"When these hungry people come out they will try to climb that tree for food and it will take much time. While Tso-a-vwits is trying to get that rabbit, we will grab Uja and get away."

Deep inside the sheep's stomach, the little grouse felt the pains coming from his own stomach. "Tso-a-vwits, I am so hungry!" he wailed over and over. "All right, all right! I'll get you something to eat." She told her baby-hearted husband. Ever so slowly, the old woman pried the sheep's ribs apart and quietly crept from their hiding place. She lifted her nose and sniffed at the cool night air. Tso-a-vwits was entranced by the smell of fresh rabbit, just as Kwani had planned, and she stealthily crept over to the tall pine. Hastily, she embraced the huge tree trying to climb but her feet slipped on the freshly peeled trunk and she fell to the ground. Looking up, she could now see the rabbit but she could not see any branches close enough to reach. Again and again she lunged at the tree as her baby-husband's muffled sobs came from inside the sheep.

Kwani watched the old woman's first few attempts, and when he was sure that she would not give up the climb, he swooped down and grabbed Uji from his hiding place. He carried the man-boy back and laid him under the sage bush where his mother had first placed him. Instantly, the man-boy was transformed back into the little sage grouse.

Kwani knew there was still great danger, however, and he flew off into the west and brought back a terrible storm. Fierce winds howled across the mountain and down the valley. Rain drops pounded into the dust of the trail and washed away his tracks so Tso-a-vwits couldn't follow him. Unfortunately, however, the old woman found eagle feathers near the sheep's carcass. Enraged, she shook her fist at the storm and screamed into the night.

"Kwani! I know you are the brother of Iowi. You are a great warrior and a terrible man! But I am not done yet. I will go to my grandfather, Togoa, and he will avenge me!"

Sun was high in the sky the next day when Tso-a-vwits came to the rattlesnake asleep on a rock. Before she could utter a word her grandfather began to shake his rattles and hissed at her. "Go back, go back, you are not wanted here, go back!"

"Grandfather, have pity on me!" she sobbed. "Kwani has stolen my husband, and now he is coming for me."

"Bahhh. You never tell me the truth. You are too ugly to have a husband."

"Grandfather, please! I cannot live without my husband."

Just then, a loud kwiiiii sounded overhead.

"Grandfather, it is *Kwani*! He has found me. Please help me!"

Rattlesnake flicked his tongue several times before answering.

"Hide, hide!" He hissed and unhinged his jaws, opening his mouth so that the old hag could climb inside. *Tso-a-vwits* climbed on down his throat and into his stomach, which made *Togoa* very sick.

"Granddaughter, you must come back up! You are making me sick!"

"No, no! I can't. *Kwani* will kill me!" cried the muffled voice of *Tso-a-vwits*.

Togoa tried to throw her up but he couldn't. He writhed in pain, retching and retching to no avail. After several minutes of struggling, he finally managed to crawl out of his own skin. *Tso-a-vwits* was imprisoned there, however, and thrashed about until she finally fell into a crevice in the rocks. *Kwani* continued to circle overhead.

"Where are you old *Tso-a-vwits*?" he shouted.

"Where are you old *Tso-a-vwits*?" she repeated his words in mockery.

Ever since that day, witches live in snake skins and hide among the rocks where they delight in taunting intruders by repeating their words. The White Man has lost the history of these ancient people but the *Numas*, Ute, know the voices of these old hags. This is the origin of the echo.

WHAT CAN WE LEARN FROM "ORIGINS OF ECHO"?

In our society, we allow animals death with dignity. We exclude them from suffering a prolonged and agonized end of life. However, we don't generally offer humans this same option. The Ute had a surprising and effective solution to this dilemma. In their society, it was customary for an aged person to go and "gather firewood" on a cold, wintry day. When far enough from camp, the elder would sit down and sing a Death Chant in order to prepare their Spirit for its journey to the Spirit World. Powell maintains that this practice was the result of fear of becoming a witch.[23] Perhaps this was factored into the decision to end life. However, most informants told me that it was to spare the viability of the village itself, so that their nomadic life would not be hampered by caring for the aged.

Powell did not fully understand this concept when he wrote of his experiences. He felt that this voluntary end of life was due to a belief that a very aged woman would turn into a *Unupits*, or witch, and be doomed to live in a snakeskin, much like Echo.

they believed [it is] better to die than to meet with such a fate. This is not only the general sentiment prevailing among the people, but great pains are taken to inculcate this belief, and it is quite common for old women to commit suicide, which they do by voluntarily starving. I once saw three old women around a fire in a deserted camp. The other members had left sometime before and these had remained behind for the purpose of dying by starvation. When I rode up to the camp they paid no attention to me but sat gazing into the fire for some time and then each one supporting herself by a staff rose to her

23   Fowler, *Anthropology of the Numa* 61.

feet and they joined in a dance which was a shuffling movement, circling around the fire. This dance was accompanied with a chant as follows:

Ai-ai Ai-ai ai-ai
   Ai-ai Ai-ai ai-ai
I'van tu'-ni-shump pa-ni-gunt
   Y-ni-shump uni-shump
      I-ai-kwa-vwan i-ai-kwa-vwan

Alas, alas, alas
   Alas, alas, alas
Here long enough have I walked the earth
   Here long enough have I walked the earth
   Enough, enough
   Let me die, let me die.

I did not know what it meant at the time, yet it made a deep impression upon my mind, for the song itself and the circumstances, and whole manner of the women was wild and weird in the extreme. When they had chanted for perhaps half an hour in this way they sat down again, mumbling something which I could not understand, and gazing in the fire. They rose again and danced, and again sat down. At last I rode on, and coming a few days afterwards to where the tribe was encamped, I made inquiry and learned that these women had remained behind for the purpose of dying by starvation and that it was considered by the rest of the tribe as being very *meritorious*.[24] [emphasis added.]

Why would the Utes consider the old women dying of starvation "meritorious" if they only wanted to avoid becoming witches? This attitude seems more in accordance with the practice of the elderly removing

---

24   Fowler, 61.

themselves when they became a burden on the band. Perhaps the Ute were mocking Powell when they told him about this "fear" of becoming witches. I have found that this is quite common when they are asked an inappropriate question. It is a subtle form of Native American humor, and the victim usually doesn't even realize he is the butt of a joke.

Story of Eagle and Frog [25]

Just as the sun is sending its eyes over the jagged mountain range, *Kwanaci* (eagle) circles in the sky four times. He slowly spirals downward and then flaps his huge wings as his feet touch the ground. He turns his head and surveys the nearby cliffs. "I am alone here in the village of my people. Why have they disappeared?"

Kwanaci walks around, bewildered, looking everywhere. Whoosh! He gives a final flap of his wings that propel him to the top of a boulder. He sits there, thinking.

"I will see about this!" And he suddenly stands up as he spots a dusty trail.

"This *kwasiv* (trail) is full of footprints. I am following my people like I follow a deer."

He bends his head over the faint path, and waddling awkwardly from side to side follows it along the summit of the cliff. The trail winds down the rocky escarpment between two fir trees. At the base, far below, he now sees the bodies of his people.

"EEEE! Why are my people lying down there, on top of each other! What shall I do?" As he wrings his hands in dismay he notices the smoke from a fire nearby. This cook fire is in the middle of an eagle's nest, and Frog is living there. Eagle walks closer to the nest. He then goes inside where he finds *Mamuch* (woman) sitting down.

"*Mamuch*, kindle a fire! I am cold!"

---

25   Transcribed and retold by Celinda Reynolds Kaelin from Powell's Mss. 794a, Part II.

Turning her head away, the woman ignores *Kwanaci*. She moves to the door, looking outside, "Well, I am NOT cold." She haughtily sniffs. Just then they both hear a jumping noise outside.

"Ahhh, there is a very beautiful man coming," she says. "He is *Paqxwani* (Frog)!"

Paqxwani saunters into the house. When he sees *Kwanaci*, he stops dead in his tracks. Looking him up and down with contempt, he gloats, saying, "*Hegh!* I am better looking than you!"

"No. I say you are rough and ugly!" *Kwanaci* responds angrily to *Paqxwani's* arrogance.

At this, *Paqxwani* takes a wooden bowl of water and looks at his reflection in it, admiring himself.

"*Kwanaci*, I say I am a beautiful man! Yellow eyes, yellow hands!"

Paqxwani then throws *Kwanaci* on his back and walks to the edge of the cliff. After he finally sits *Kwanaci* down, he studies him carefully and rubs his eyes. He doesn't want to admit it but *Kwanaci* is so beautiful that he is dazzled, so he rubs his eyes again. Then he sits down and stares long and hard at *Kwanaci*.

"There was a woman sitting with you when I came in the house. She was in love with you!" *Paqxwani* jealously accuses *Kwanaci*.

"Ehhhh. A girl always does that way. I only came here to find my people. They are all gone!"

"Ehhhh. Don't worry. Those eagles nearby will fly again after a while. But I am used to walking on rocks." And to prove his point, *Paqxwani* stands up and struts around.

"*Kwanaci*, you can look at rocks, but you are awkward when you walk and you can't really walk on rocks like I can." As he says this an evil look comes into *Paqxwani's* eyes and he wickedly smiles at *Kwanaci*.

"Would you like to have a closer look at your people down there below?"

"*Euh!* As you say, we will do. It shall be done." *Kwanaci* sadly replies and, standing up, he climbs onto *Paqxwani's* back.

Paqxwani carries him to the edge of the cliff. Kwanaci climbs down, and they stand side by side looking at all of the dead eagles below. Suddenly *Paqxwani* lunges and grabs the eagle with both hands.

"Hold on! Hold on! You will fall!" At this, *Paqxwani* throws *Kwanaci* over the cliff! The eagle falls and falls. Finally, just before he hits the rocks below, he begins to flap his wings. With great swoops he circles higher and higher to the top of the cliff. *Paqxwani* is still intently looking over the cliff. Eagle lands silently, just behind frog. He then grabs him and throws him over the cliff. Frog lands far below, in a pond of mud and water.

"Ehhhh, my friend. Now you will live there far below and so will your children. This is your punishment for what you have done to my people."

WHAT CAN WE LEARN FROM "EAGLE AND FROG"?

There are a couple of aspects to this legend that I find particularly interesting. First, again, is the subtle use of Ute humor in the word *kutch* for eagle. The second point is the insight that it provides on the excellent tracking abilities of Ute scouts.

In 1868, John Wesley Powell, his wife Emma, and three guides wintered on the White River in northwestern Colorado at a spot now called Powell Bottoms. The Northern Ute bands of Chief Douglas and Antero were encamped nearby, and Powell seized the opportunity to record ethnographical data on the Ute. For some reason, Powell's informant uses the word *kutch* for eagle in the original transcription of this story. However, *kutch* is the Ute word for buffalo. Eagle is *kwanaci*. Sometimes Ute informants would do this purposely in order to trace the source of a story retold. Clifford told me that he could tell the family origin of any legend just by the manner in which it was told. But perhaps, as in the previous story, Powell's informants were gently mocking him again.

The following anecdote also calls to mind an experience that Powell had with a Paiute (relatives of the Ute) guide and his expertise at following a trail as Eagle did.

While we were passing along the road to Tokerville [Toquerville] Chu-ar-ru-um-pik noticed some Indian tracks [on the] side of the road. Pausing a moment he looked toward me and said, "Three Indians have passed this way this morning going toward Washington – an old man, a woman and a boy." I looked for a moment but saw only what appeared to me to be three or four moccasin prints in the sand. "How do you know?" said I. "How can you tell that an old man has passed?" He alighted from his horse, bent down by the tracks and putting his finger upon one said, "This is the old man," then pointing to another "this is his track again, and again." Then calling my attention to the irregularity in the length of the steps he said, "An old man walks so; a Nuints [young man, literally 'Indian'] walks with regularity." This was satisfactory to me. "But how do you know a squaw has passed?" "By the shape of the moccasins," replied he. "But how can you distinguish the squaw's from the boy?" "The squaw has followed the trail, and her moccasins are a different shape." We passed along a few rods farther and Chuarrumpik remarked, "Here the boy tried to shoot a chipmunk." "How can you tell?" said I. He called my attention to where the tracks of the boy had left the trail and then showed me how he determined this by the position of the feet when in the act of shooting or drawing a bow. Anxious to know how he determined that the game was a chipmunk, I said, "No Chuarrumpik, I think it was a rabbit." "Kuch!" said he. "No rabbits here; this is not the place for rabbits; rabbits live down in the brush; chipmunks live here." It was an argument I could not refute.

A few moments after he remarked, "They passed when the sun was there," indicating the place where the sun would be at about 8 o'clock. "How do you know?" said I. "The wind has not blown the sand into the tracks. Last night you remember the wind blew. Had they passed yesterday their tracks would have been partially filled with sand; had they passed early this morning the rabbits and chipmunks would have trodden in their tracks. Chipmunk goes abroad early in the morning. He is now in his wickiup; the rabbit also." A few minutes more he remarked, "They have gone to Washington for wheat, or rather to glean in the fields." "Why do you think so?" "The Mormons," said he, "at Washington are now cutting their wheat. The Indian corn at Tokerville is not ripe. The Pai Utes have but little to eat. They want wheat very much. I think they have gone to glean in the Mormon fields."[26]

---

26   Fowler, *Anthropology of the Numa* 65-66.

Sunawiv and Grizzly Bear[27]

I n the days before there were mountains or streams or forests, there were no people either. There was only the earth, the sky, the sun, and the clouds. *Sunawiv* (Great Spirit) lived in the center of the sky. He/She lived all alone. There were no other living beings.

27   Celinda R. Kaelin, *Pikes Peak Backcountry* (Caxton Press, 1999), 10-11.

"You, *Tava*, I command you to appear every
morning and travel across the sky to the west! You
must bring light and warm the earth, for I think I will do
something."

And so *Tava* obediently climbed onto the horizon
each morning and began his journey.

"You, *Muatago*! You will be the shadow of *Tava*, and
follow him around at the end of day. You will give only
pale light in the darkness, for I think I will do something."

"Now, *Tununiri*, you will beat your drum and
flash your light to bring the rain, for I think that I will do
something."

Sunawiv sat and thought and thought, but soon
grew tired and lonely.

"I must see new things. I must do new things." Then
He/She looked around and saw a great stone. *Sunawiv*
slowly rolled the boulder over the floor to the center of
the sky and then turned it round and round until it cut
a hole. Then He/She worked some more until the hole
was larger and larger and He/She could look down at the
earth below.

"*Towaoc*! This is good!" He/She exclaimed, looking
through the big hole in the blue sky. Now, He/She
gathered dirt and stones from his place in the sky and
poured them through the hole. Then He/She gathered
the snow and the rain and also poured them through this
big hole onto the pile of dirt and stones.

After a while *Sunawiv* looked down at the great
mountain, *Tava* (Pikes Peak), which He/She had built with
the dirt and rocks and snow and rain.

"*Aieee*! I want to make this place beautiful!" And so
He/She gathered trees and plants and flowers and placed
them on his mountain. Now, *Tava* peered through the
hole in the sky and his long arrows of light warmed the
mountain, melting the snow. This water ran down the
Peak and made the streams and in some places where

there was a hole the water gathered together and made great lakes.

"*Tava* and *Tununiri*! I want you to give your gifts of light and water to the trees and plants and flowers. I want you to help them grow and spread."

Now *Sunawiv* was pleased. Every day, *Sunawiv* came down from his/her home in the sky and walked in the beautiful meadows among the flowers or in the forests among the singing birds.

"May I come with you?" *Shin-au-am*, his/her daughter begged for permission. She often came with him to visit this mountain. One day, while her father was busy in the sky, she walked along a stream gathering flowers. *Quiagat* (Grizzly Bear) saw *Shin-au-am*."Who is this beautiful woman? I will make her my wife!" Animals still had magical powers in these times, so *Quiagat* changed himself into a handsome warrior.

Night after night he waited until *Sunawiv's* daughter came down to the stream for water. Then his fingers moved quickly over the five holes of his flute, while his love song played its magic on the beautiful girl. Finally, on the fourth day, he stepped from behind a tall pine tree. The tall, dark warrior smiled at *Shin-au-am*. "Come, share my blanket!" She smiled, and shyly walked into his arms as he drew the blanket around them both. Now they were married.

Their children are the Ute People, the People of the Bear. Great Spirit was angry with Grizzly Bear, though, and commanded that from that day forward he would have to walk on all four legs instead of two, like a human being.

WHAT CAN WE LEARN FROM "SUNAWIV AND GRIZZLY BEAR"?

This legend provides some insight on the reason that Bear is so sacred to the Ute People. They call themselves "People of the Bear," and Clifford taught that Bear was their relative. Therefore, it was taboo among the Ute to eat bear meat. This changed after the Utes were placed on reservations. With the government's emphasis on making Christians of the Ute people, this taboo is no longer adhered to except by truly traditional Utes such as Clifford. Anthropologists will tell you that without a skull it is very difficult to tell the difference between the skeleton of a bear and a human. Clifford put it succinctly when he asked, "You White People think that you came from monkeys. I'd rather come from a Bear!"

Each spring, the Ute People celebrate the awakening of *Quiagat* from his long winter's sleep with the Bear Dance. Clifford explains it this way.

> Mother Earth wakes up from her winter sleep in spring. That is why you begin to see rocks rolling down the hill side, mud slides and streams choked with water. And the winds come alive again, too, because the earth is stretching and moving as she awakens.[28]

This ceremony is unique to Ute culture, and is a powerful time of healing and bringing the People together. It is held in a brush covered arena, the *avinkwep*, shaped like a horse shoe, with the opening to the east.

The origin of the dance was explained by the tale of a hunter who saw a bear dancing back and forth to a pine tree, and on his return home the hunter taught his people

---

28   Author Interview, Clifford Duncan, 4/22/1998

to do the dance.[29]

In homage to this vision/dream, the men line up on the west side and the women face them on the east, about four feet apart. As the music begins, they dance forward and backward, just as the bear did. Music is provided by a drum made from a sheet of corrugated metal placed over a four-by-eight foot pit. One end of a notched stick, the *w'ni thokunup* (a morache), rests on the metal and resonates as a stick slides up and down the notches. The sound is remarkably similar to thunder or the growling of a bear. Again, Clifford clarifies the importance of the Bear Dance:

> White People say the Bear Dance is only social, like a primitive mating dance. This is wrong. Bear Dance is a celebration of all life. Like the bear that comes back to life with spring, so do the people. They have stayed in tipis all winter, and are ready to return outdoors but there is much danger from wild animals. Bear rolls over with the first thunder of spring, and this is time to collect herbs that grow along the ground. This herb then is used to bless all things that crawl – snakes, etc.–and ask them to be at peace with the *Nuntz* [Ute] and protect them as they collect food.[30]

Ethnographer Ann Smith's informants reported that it was formerly a custom on the last day of the dance to have a man and woman appear in the arena wearing a bearskin robe, impersonating the male and female bear.

> When these two are dancing the usual song is *kata pikaa paiitaci iya*. These two lines are repeated several times. They mean: He is singing. His fur is swaying as he dances. He is going to get away with the Buffalo's

29   Smith, *Ethnography of the Northern Ute* 221
30   Author Interview, Clifford Duncan, 3/10/1998

wife. Grass like cattail leaves, only round, that is what the bear is going to eat. Going down a willow-lined creek, the bear is going down to eat this grass.[31]

Historian Robert Emmitt tells us that if a dancer fell during the dance, special measures were required before the dance could continue. This was necessitated because the fall may have been caused by evil. Therefore, it required the services of a man with strong medicine power – the power of bear medicine, a *m'sut t'quigat*.

... [the Medicine Man] came with the *w'ni thokunup* [morache] and stick to drive away the bad spirits that had made the fall. When a dancer fell, the music stopped, and the fallen one did not move until the *m'sut t'quigat* had brought the *w'ni thokunup* and stick, making motions to push the evil out of his feet and chase it off toward the sky.[32]

31   Smith, *Ethnography of the Northern Utes* 220
32   Robert Emmitt, *The Last War Trail: The Utes and the Settlement of Colorado* (Oklahoma UP, 1954) 35-39.

Coyote and the Seven Stars of the Pleiades[33]

A long time ago, a widow had five daughters and one son. One day she decided to marry again and the stepfather came to live with them. On a blustery day in November, *Yohowitz* left his new family to hunt elk. When he was out of sight, Coyote scratched himself and then put *turasanagovi* (gumweed) on the wounds to make it look like he had been shot. When he got back home he told his family that he had been in a battle.

"I am mortally wounded and I don't have long to live." He gasped, writhing in pain. "After I die you must go to the camp over in the next valley. When you get there look for a man on a white horse. He will be better than the other men. Oldest Daughter, you must marry this man." And with this, Coyote's last breath seemed to leave his body.

As he had told her to do, *Yohowitz's* wife placed his corpse on a high platform on some poles. This would help him to have a quick journey to the Spirit World. She and the children turned and started back to their village. As they walked, the little boy looked over his shoulder.

"No," his mother sternly admonished. "You must not look back."

"But, Mother, I can see him falling off the poles!"

"Do not look back! Remember he said he would do you injury if you looked back."

"But, Mother, he is crawling away!"

33   Uintah-Ouray Ute Tribe 72-73, 89.

When they got to their tipi, the mother cried and cut her hair as a sign of mourning.

Several weeks later the little boy came running to his mother.

"I saw the man on the white horse! I saw the man that stepfather told us about! He came galloping into our village just now!"

They were all excited and ran to the center of their village to see for themselves. There was a handsome man riding a fine white horse. He was wearing a mountain lion skin with its long tail hanging down the back. He did not look like Coyote at all.

"Bring your brother-in-law." The young son obeyed his mother and went to bring their *Yohowitz* home. The boy was suspicious, however, and looked at him from the corner of his eye. Nonetheless, the man on the white horse married the oldest daughter just as the stepfather said he would.

The next morning the woman told her son, "You must take your new brother-in-law hunting for rabbits."

The boy and the man set out early in the morning and were soon walking carefully among the fragrant sage bushes. They both carried long clubs and poked them into the rabbit holes to get them to come out. The boy found one very large hole to one side of the man and bent down on his knees to shove his stick deeply into the hole. As he did this, he happened to look over at his new brother-in-law. Coyote was leaning over the other side of the hole with his mouth open, waiting for the rabbit to come out.

Why, this man has seven holes in his teeth, just as my stepfather did! When he realized this, the boy jumped up as quickly as he could and ran for home.

"Mother! Mother!" He was breathless from the run and his excitement. "That man has seven holes in his teeth just as our stepfather did! He did not die at all!"

"Ahhh. Now I see," moaned the mother. "He planned

71

this all along. That's why he told us about the man on the white horse! All he wanted was to marry his stepdaughter. *Aaaiiiii!*" And she wailed and pulled her hair in anguish.

"Where can we go? How will we get away? He will try to find us, Mother! We must run and hide!" The children were all crying and frightened. Then they heard Coyote's voice.

"I will find you! You can't hide from me!" They could hear him coming closer.

"Children, we must be calm and we must think," whispered the mother. After a few minutes, they carefully climbed down a hole one by one and then went underground for a short distance. When they came out, they floated up into the sky where they live to this day. That is why you can see seven stars up in the sky. The last star is the little brother. He always looked back.

Yohowitz followed their tracks until they disappeared. He looked all around but could see no one. Coyote stood there puzzled. But the boy thought, *I wish my father would look at me.* As soon as he thought this Coyote looked up and saw them.

"*Ah hah!* You are now stars in the sky! Everyone will call you Coyote's Family."

The woman answered, "Yes, but we are safe from you. You will have to stay there below. People on earth will call you Coyote. Every evening, where ever there is a campfire, you will prowl around looking for your family. At night you will howl at the stars. You will be Coyote."

WHAT CAN WE LEARN FROM "COYOTE AND THE SEVEN STARS"?

I think that this story gives one of the most interesting insights into Ute cosmology – their connection to the Star People. When Clifford and I were traveling in South America with the World Council of Elders, the Mayan priests led us in a powerful ceremony at the Temple of the Jaguar in Tikal. Afterward, in the dark tropical sky above the temple, a UFO zigzagged above our heads. I was awestruck by this bright point of yellow-white light that seemed to be communicating with us.

"Yes, it is our relatives from the Pleiades," explained one of the Mayan priests. "Long ago, as explained in the *Popul Vuh*, Pleiadians came to earth and interbred with humans. *Balam*, Jaguar, is our name for the Pleiades."

Much to my surprise Clifford chimed in, "Yes, the Ute People have a similar teaching. We come from the Pleiades, and we honored them at every encampment."

He then continued to explain this remarkable insight.

As above, so below. This teaching of the Utes also applies to the *Soniawi* (Seven Stars)[34], what we call the Pleiades. Each time the Ute People set up a new camp, they did so in the crescent shape of the Pleiades. Their crescent-shaped village opens to the east. In the center, where the brightest two stars seem to dance out of the crescent, stand the Medicine Man's tipi and the Chief's tipi. Just beyond them is the Medicine Wheel. This was done so that the People will always remember that they come from the Pleiades.[35]

---

34   *Ute Dictionary* (Ute Press of the Southern Ute Tribe, 1979) 271.

35   Author Interview, Clifford Duncan, 8/5/2000

Coyote Steals Fire [36]

Along time ago, *Yohowitz* (Coyote) lived in a large village where he was chief. His people were always cold, however, because they had no fire. Instead, they gathered large, flat rocks and piled them together. The sun warmed them during the day, but when evening came they were only slightly warm. Early the next morning, *Yohowitz* threw water on them and they steamed, and this made them hotter.

Late one night, Coyote was laying on his buffalo blanket in his tipi. Suddenly, a bright red ember floated down in front of him. Smoke from this fire had carried the ember up, through the smoke hole, and the winds had carried it back into Coyote's bed. He quickly snatched it up and hid it away. Then he went outside and called all of his head men for a council. When they had gathered in his tipi, he pulled the ember out.

"This is what I want you to look at. What do you think? Do you know what it is? Where does it come from? I wish that you all speak."

His words were only met with silence, however, so *Yohowitz* growled at them.

"I do not want you to do that. I want you to talk. In order that we may find this out, I wish you all not to be silent."

His head men lowered their heads and looked at one another. Finally, *Muupuci* (Owl) responded.

"We do not know what this is."

Yohowitz pursed his lips and pointed to *Muupuci*

---

36   Unitah-Ouray Ute Tribe 13-21.

with them (it is impolite to point with a finger). "I select you; bring very many Owls."

He repeated this command to each of his head men, instructing Eagle, Crow, Grouse, Hummingbird, and Tarantula Hawk Moth to bring all of their people of the bird nation for a great council. He gave one of the men special instructions

"My friend, go to the river and get reeds. Bring them here."

This man hurried off to the riverbank, and soon returned with an armful of reeds. Coyote took a big stick and pounded them until the sun was going down, when they were fully shredded. After darkness came, *Yohowitz* called all of his head men again. When they had gathered in his tipi, he began to pile the shredded reeds into a heap. Then he told them to go home. They asked one another, "Why does *Yohowitz* do that?"

When *Yohowitz* was alone again, he took out his paint bag and rubbed dark blue paint on the reeds until they turned blue. Then he rubbed even more, and the shredded reeds turned black. They looked like human hair. Coyote's mind was spinning so fast that he could hardly sleep that night.

As the sun rose the next morning, *Yohowitz* placed the blackened, shredded reeds on his head and called his head men together a third time. He stood before them, with long black tendrils of reed trailing to the ground. He did not look like Coyote, and his men were puzzled.

"Who knows why I am doing this? What do you think?"

No one answered for a very long time. They thought that this was a trick question because *Yohowitz* must certainly know what he was doing.

"We do not know what this is." And having said this, they all went home again.

When they were out of sight, Coyote took off his

bark hair, wrapped it up and put it away. He was anxious for all of the people to gather for the council, and sent scouts to watch from the hill tops. His mind continued to race round and round this thing that he had found. As the different tribes finally began to arrive, *Yohowitz* ordered them to stay in the tipis of his own people, and not to camp separately.

"Eat quickly and come to council with me." Coyote had joined three large tipis together to make one large council tipi. All of the tribes gathered there at nightfall, and sat in rows of circles in order to hear *Yohowitz'* words. He placed his treasured ember on something, and then sent it around from one man to another.

"Do you know what this thing is? Do you know where it came from? Did it come from above?" He was annoyed when no one answered, but continued, "I intend to hunt up this thing. I shall find out from where it comes, from what tribe it is, or whether it is from the sky. I want you to search, looking where each of you thinks best. That is why I called you. We will start in the morning."

"Very well, we follow your advice. We will go behind you; we wish that you lead us. That is why we came here."

Still, they were puzzled. "Which way would you go?" they asked one another. "I do not know," they replied to each other.

Yohowitz heard their confusion. "There is mostly a considerable wind from the West; it does not come from any other direction." He clarified, "I think that is where this thing came from. That is what I think. Let us go there." And with that, he placed his bark hair in a carrying thong and they began their journey. They traveled until darkness fell around them. Coyote had nothing further to say as they made camp. They resumed their journey at daylight, and continued this way for three days. The third night they camped at the base of a mountain. Just as the sun rose the next day they climbed to the summit.

"Which way shall we go?" *Yohowitz* asked his people. No one answered so he carefully scanned the horizon. He saw another mountain so far away that it looked like smoke. "We will go straight to that mountain there." Having decided a course of action, they climbed back down from their vantage point and camped on the far side of the mountain. *Yohowitz* was silent all the way but around camp that evening he finally volunteered. "I think the place that the ember came from is much farther. I think it is near the mountain that we saw from the summit. My friends, I shall ask for scouts to go ahead." When he finished speaking, his people picked up their loads and continued across a level plain over the next two days. They stopped, finally, at the base of a new mountain range. "We will stay here. Tomorrow I wish some of you to go away to look, searching all over the world for the source of the ember."

Coyote walked through the village the next morning, stopping in front of *Sigwanaci*'s (Red - Tailed Hawk's) tipi.

"You, my friend, will climb high in the sky today and search as far as you can see."

The entire camp watched for Hawk all day, and ran toward him as he landed in the twilight. *Yohowitz* reached him first and asked breathlessly, "What did you see, my friend?"

Sigwanaci sadly shook his head. "I saw nothing. I became tired. I could not fly higher. I could not see the edge of the earth. I was not high enough."

"Yes," said *Yohowitz*, gazing off in the far distance. He sat on a rock and thought and thought. All at once he sprang to his feet and rushed to the tipi of *Kwanaci* (Eagle).

"You go," he said to the great bird, who sadly shook his head.

"I do not think I will reach there. But I will try."
With a great flapping of his wing he lifted off and spiraled
higher and higher toward the sun until he disappeared
from sight. Two days later there was a great *whoosh* and
Kwanaci landed at the edge of the village. Again, *Yohowitz*
rushed to greet him, arriving ahead of the others.

"I could go no farther. It was hard to go farther, I
was tired. I saw nothing. Only I saw that the earth looked
a little smoky."

All of the head men looked around at one
another, puzzled by what they must do next. *Muutataaci*
(Hummingbird) darted back and forth above their heads.
Rose light from the setting sun bounced off of his shiny
wings and head, and in unison they called out to Coyote.

"*Yohowitz*, send *Muutataaci*! Send *Muutataaci*! He
can do better than the eagle. Each winter he flies far, far
south."

Coyote walked up to the tiny bird that had landed
on a piñon branch. "*Muutataaci*, try what you can do, my
friend. I think you can do something."

Hummingbird made no answer, but sat silently,
thinking. After several minutes, he darted into the air.
He moved so quickly that no one could see where he had
gone. Day after day passed and he did not return. Coyote
anxiously prowled the camp.

"Can you see *Muutataaci* returning?" his voice was
high and tense.

But no one had seen the little bird. Again he asked,
"Has he not come back yet? Search about! See what has
become of him; perhaps he has gone to sleep."

The entire village spread out and looked in every
bush and tree but could not find Hummingbird. Night
came and the exhausted villagers returned just in time
to hear something buzzing. They all gathered around the
little winged one.

Coyote said, "Well, *Muutataaci*, how far were you?"

Hummingbird only sat still and said nothing. After a long silence, he answered.

"Very well, I will begin to speak now. At the edge of the earth and the sky, where they are together, I saw something standing. It was very far away. Something was there; I do not think we can reach it. It was a dark thing standing up, and the top was bent over. That was all I saw." The little bird hung his head and heaved a great sigh.

"That is what I thought one of you would see," Coyote replied. "That is what we are going for. It is from this that the thing came which I found." And Coyote smiled as he continued. "*Muutataaci*, what you say makes my heart feel good." He walked among his people, still smiling. He could not sit still, but passed through the village several times before announcing, "We will start and go a distance, then camp again for the night."

Dew from the grass clung to their leggings as the village began to move the next morning. In single file they followed one another across the next mountain ridge and down the other side. They camped that night at the base of the mountain and then traveled on another day where they made camp on a wide plain.

Early the next morning they climbed yet another mountain and made camp that evening on its other side. Again Coyote sent scouts to see how close they were to the dark thing standing up with its head bent over. Eagle was the first to go, and when he returned Coyote questioned him closely.

"*Kwanaci*, what did you see?"

Eagle shook his head and ruffled his feathers. "I saw nothing. It is very dangerous to go up. It is very difficult."

Coyote then turned to Hummingbird, "Go again, *Muutataaci*! See how far from it we are now." At this command, Hummingbird zipped into the air and was soon out of sight. It was not long before he returned. Coyote and the villagers excitedly gathered around him.

"I saw three mountain ranges this side of it. We are approaching it."

Coyote was anxious to start again, so they traveled all day and camped at the foot of the next mountain. The next day they crossed over it and made camp on its far side. Now the pace became more urgent, with Coyote leading the way over yet another mountain range. Still, another chain of peaks loomed ahead.

"We will go on again to the foot of that mountain," Coyote assured his people. "That mountain is the last one. We will stop here and wash and become clean and dress. I think there are people there; therefore wash and decorate yourselves."

Each of the headmen did as Coyote directed, and put on their finest regalia, feathers, and paint. Coyote also took great pains with his appearance. He placed the shredded bark in his hair, and spread it all out so that it looked like his own hair. He then parted it in the middle and braided both sides so that the braids fell to his feet. He then wrapped the braids in bark. As he was finishing these preparations he turned to Eagle.

"Kwanaci, my friend, go up again and see how close we are."

Eagle returned with his report in a few minutes, "We are not very far away now. I saw what Hummingbird saw. We are near!"

Coyote led his people to the top of the mountain and gathered them about him. He counted them out and divided them into twenties. "Each band of twenty is to go to one tipi. I will go to the tipi of the head chief with twenty of my head men." They followed Coyote down the mountain and gathered around him again before going into the village. Coyote now shared his plan with them.

"We have burned nothing before now. Our fire was not fire. We have come to fire now. We will stay here two days. It is the fire for which we have come. We will take it away from them. They will have none left here. Where the origin of the fire is, there they will have no more fire. We will take it to the place where we live and we will possess it in our own land. I will use this hair of mine to take it away from them. I will deceive these people that have the fire. I will tell them that we wish them to make a large fire. I think that is the best way to do it. What do you think?"

His band answered in unison, "Yes, that is the right way."

Since they all agreed, Coyote continued detailing his strategy, "Before we take the fire away from them, I shall whoop twice; keep apart by yourselves, ready to go. Do not tell them why we come here. Keep it to yourselves. All of you take my advice. Follow it. Do not forget it. We have not the right kind of fire to use, but after we take this we shall possess fire in our land. We will run away. No one of us will stay. I do not think that they will let us escape easily, but they will pursue us and attack us and try to kill us."

Each of his headmen nodded in approval so Coyote walked to the edge of the group and led his men down into the village. He rattled the dew claws hanging by the door of the first tipi and stuck his head in.

"Where is the lodge of your chief?" When the old woman pointed to the tipi in the center Coyote thanked her and added, "That is where I will live."

Coyote greeted the strange chief, "My friend, I am nearly exhausted from traveling."

"Very well. You have reached my camp. It is good," and the chief spread his right arm to show his village. "Here are my people. You can go to their tipis. You can divide and stay with them."

In the morning Coyote called to his people to gather at the lodge of the chief. After they crowded into the tipi and arranged themselves on the buffalo robes Coyote stood and addressed the chief.

"Well, my friend, I traveled. I came only to see you. I desire that you all make a dance for me on the second night. I came very far and I wish to see a dance; that is what all my people like."

His host responded, "It is good; I am glad that you came for a dance. I like it. I will make a big dance for you where I live."

That night the chief sent his crier through the village, "Make a dance for these people! Make a dance for these people! They like to see our way of dancing. *Yohowitz* asks that you all put out your fires when you dance. *Yohowitz* asks for only one large fire."

The people poured water on all the fires, including each fire in their tipi. All the people gathered at the big fire, including the women and children. It was a large village and no one was left in their tipi.

Coyote stood before the large fire and said approvingly, "Let us keep up this fire all the night." He took his carrying thong off his shoulder and opened it. Then he opened the bundle with the blackened bark and spread it out. When he placed it on his head the people thought he was adorning himself for the dance. Coyote danced and danced without resting. He kept up his pace until the sun began to light the eastern sky and then he let out the first of his signal whoops. At this everyone stopped dancing and looked at Coyote.

"I do not mean anything," his voice full of innocence. "I only whooped to show that I like this very well; to show that I like this dance. I never had this kind of dance in my land. It makes my heart good to see all these women and fine girls and your way of dancing. I mean nothing wrong."

"Very well," they said and went back to dancing.

More and more light painted the sky as the sun climbed the horizon, and once again Coyote moved close to the fire and gave a second signal whoop. At this, all of

84

his men separated from the villagers and prepared to flee. When he saw they were in place, Coyote took off his bark hair. Holding it with both hands, he hit the fire and put it out. His hair now had all of the fire, so Coyote dashed to his circle of waiting men. They ran as fast as they could, their feet pounding the earth like stampeding horses.

"That is what he intended to do," yelled the outraged chief. "Now, let us kill all his people."

Coyote was already at the top of the first ridge when he looked back and saw the chief and his men in close pursuit. He was beginning to tire, so he came up close to Eagle and handed him the fire.

"You can run fast! Take this my friend." Eagle took the precious fire and ran as fast as he could until he grew tired, then he handed it to Hummingbird.

"*Muutataaci*, I am nearly exhausted. You carry this for a while."

Coyote now dropped to the rear of his fleeing people and cautioned them.

"If any of you are tired and are exhausted, hide somewhere. In this way you will save your lives. When we get over this adventure, we shall be safe. In this way we will be saved by hiding from our pursuer."

As they ran, each of the different bird people continued to hand the fire to another as they tired. Hummingbird handed the fire to Tarantula Hawk Moth.

"I am nearly exhausted. Take it, my friend. I think you are good yet." Tarantula Hawk Moth gathered the fire bundle in his long, black, hairy hands and then threw it onto his back where the fire permanently colored his wings iridescent orange. Behind him, the slower birds, like Hawk, were beginning to tire and looked for hiding places. Coyote looked over his shoulder once more and saw their pursuers drawing closer.

"*Kwanacici*," he called to Chicken Hawk, "come closer. You are the swiftest of us all. You must carry the fire now." When Chicken Hawk began to tire, Coyote took the fire himself and ran, encouraging the others, "Run, run as hard as you can!" After a few miles, Coyote was gasping for breath, "Someone! Take it quickly!" Hummingbird buzzed by his head and grabbed the fire from his hands. "Stop!" Coyote yelled. "The fire is nearly out!" Hummingbird angrily flung the fire back to Coyote then went into the branches of a piñon where he hid, sulking. Only four were now left to carry the fire: Coyote, Eagle, Chicken Hawk, and Tarantula Hawk Moth. The rest had all scattered and hidden from the pursuer.

Coyote ran as fast as he could, but the chief and his people were steadily closing the distance between them. Eagle and the other two became exhausted and hid, leaving the burden of saving the fire to Coyote. He ran over the crest of a small hill and climbed into a hole on the other side. He covered the opening with a stone and hid inside, guarding the tiny spark of fire that was left. When the coast was clear, he climbed out and changed his direction, zigzagging up a nearby ravine. His pursuers caught sight of his maneuvers, and rushed to close in on him again. After a while, they began to tire.

"Let him go," said the chief. "We will cause rain and then snow. We will make a hard storm and freeze him to death and put the fire out."

Dark clouds gathered and rain fell in sheets as Coyote ran and ran. Still it rained until he landed in knee-deep water with each step. Coyote began to despair.

"I am carrying this fire now and perhaps it will go out soon. I wish I could find someone, some animal living in this land." At that moment, he saw a small hill with a few cedars. He thought that he might find shelter under their branches. Just before he reached the cedar trees he saw Black-tailed Rabbit sitting right in the water. Coyote thrust the fire at Rabbit.

"Quick, *Tavooch*! I have been getting fire from far

away. I have it now. It is this fire that has brought me into difficulty, which has caused this rain. This fire will kill me. I am tired. You should know something. You should do something. You should know how to save this fire. Perhaps you do know some way. *Tavooch*, my friend, you must do it. I think you know something."

Rabbit took the fire and put it right under himself as Coyote watched in horror.

"Do not do that! You are in the water. It will go out. You will put the fire out!" howled Coyote. So Rabbit handed the fire back, but it was now burning brighter than before.

"Well, *Tavooch*! Take it, keep it."

"No," said Rabbit. "There is a cave in the rock over there where you can go in. It will be good."

Coyote raced over to the cave. Once his eyes adjusted to the darkness, he looked around and found some dry sagebrush and some dry cedar just lying about. He stood staring at the wood and thinking. Suddenly he understood. "I will make a fire out of this." He heaped the sagebrush into a pile and placed the small burning ember under it, then gently blew. Next, he turned to the cedar.

"I shall use you," he said to Cedar. "I will make a large fire out of you. You will be burned."

He heaped the cedar on top of the sagebrush, and soon had a roaring fire. He was soaking wet and he shivered from the cold but the fire soon warmed him. After a while the rain stopped but then the west wind began and carried snow with it. The people intended this in order to freeze Coyote dead. West Wind whistled and shrieked and soon froze all of the water lying on the ground. Coyote's cave was now surrounded by a sea of ice, but he was nice and cozy by the fire and was soon fast asleep. *I do not think that I will freeze to death.* As he slept, he dreamed that all the clouds had gone and that the sky was clear. When he awoke in the morning, he walked outside and saw that the sky was clear, but everything was still ice. Soon South Wind came and melted the frozen crust, so Coyote went back inside his cave.

He took a piece of dry sagebrush and bored a hole into it. He filled this cavity with coals of fire and then carefully closed it over. *I can safely carry the fire this way,* he thought. Coyote then tucked the fire under his belt and continued on his way home without even looking back. When he arrived at his village he set the sagebrush tube with the fire down on the ground.

"Come and see what I have brought you!" he called to the village.

When everyone had gathered round, Coyote took an arrow point and bored a small hole into the stick. Next, he whittled a hard piece of greasewood.

"Now watch this and you will see something." And with that, he had two men hold the sagebrush securely to the ground while he bored it with the greasewood. He carefully collected the borings and gently placed them in a mound of fine, dry grass. Then he sent several gentle breaths into the mound until a flame erupted. "This dry pine nut will be burned hereafter. Dry cedar will also be burned," he proclaimed. "Take fire into all the tipis. I shall throw away the rocks. There will be fire in every tipi."

WHAT CAN WE LEARN FROM "COYOTE STEALS FIRE"?

I find several aspects of Coyote stealing fire from the Thunder Beings especially intriguing. The first relates to the origins of the Ute Nation and again hints at a possible link to their ancestors.

As related above, Coyote sets up a procedure for extinguishing all of the fires in the tipis and the village, allowing only a large ceremonial fire. It is from this ceremonial fire that he steals the source of fire for all people. This is remarkably similar to the Mayan and Aztec New Fire Ceremony.

As we discussed in the last chapter, the Mayans (as well as the Aztecs), like the Utes[37], believe that they are descendants of beings from the Pleiades. Each November, as the Pleiades star cluster crosses through the center of the heavens, the Mayans celebrate their New Fire Ceremony. A description of the Mayan New Fire Ceremony reads as follows:

On this night they lit the new fire, and before they lit it they put out the fires of all the provinces, towns and houses...when they saw that the [Pleiades] passed the zenith...[and all the people were] waiting to see the new fire, that was the signal that the world would continue on.[38]

The Aztec ceremony was quite similar.

Aztec people ritually extinguished all fires...a procession of Fire Priests and a captive warrior solemnly filed out of Tenochtitlan toward the sacred Hill of the star...[where]they watched the Pleiades

---

37   Author Interview, Clifford Duncan, 8/5/2000.
38   Adrian G. Gilbert and Maurice M. Cotterell, *The Mayan Prophecies* (Barns & Noble Books, 1995) 130.

nearing the zenith...and kindled a fire...[This] New Fire was then used to rekindle all the main fires throughout the city.[39]

Could this legend of Coyote stealing fire be an echo of the Mayan or Aztec New Fire Ceremony? If so, does this legend provide another link to the Anasazi culture at Chaco? Both archaeologists and anthropologists agree that the Hopi are descended from the Anasazi. However, they have generally ignored the fact that the Hopi and the Ute shared a common language until about 1300 CE. This was discussed in some detail in Chapter 1.

On a more practical level, this legend provides procedures for starting a fire that are remarkably similar to those recorded by ethnographer Ann Smith from 1936-37 field notes by Sapir.

All informants recalled the use of the hearth and drill. A large piece of sagebrush wood was smoothed off on one side with a stone and two small holes were made in the center of the smoothed side. A greasewood stick, sharpened at the end, and about a foot long, was used for the drill. Sagebrush bark, rubbed until it was soft and shredded, was used for tinder. The hearth was held down with both feet and the drill was rotated between both hands until a spark emerged.[40]

Coyote Steals Fire is a fine example of how these legends speak on many levels. In this story we not only have an entertaining tale but also instructions for making fire, as well as an historic preservation of the Mayan-Aztec New Fire Ceremony.

39   John Major Jenkins, *Maya Cosmogenesis 2012* (Bear & Company, 1998) 82-83.
40   Smith, *Ethnography of the Northern Utes* 68.

Coyote Obtains Pine Nuts[41]

A long time ago, *Yahowitz* (Coyote) fell into a trance as though he were dead. His people placed him in the center of a circle and then danced around him. His older brother, *Sunawiv* (Wolf), doctored him with an eagle feather in order to call his *patanuwici*[42] (spirit) back from the Spirit World. At last he revived.

"*Yahowitz*, what happened? What did you see?" Wolf anxiously questioned his little brother.

Coyote staggered to his feet and rubbed his eyes. "I smelled something sweet. I smelled piñon nuts. But I don't know where the smell was coming from. We must send all of the people out to find this wonderful food!"

"No," replied Wolf. "I think I will do something." And then he sat on his haunches silently thinking. After a few minutes a strong wind begins to blow from the east, *tapai mawisika*[43]. Wolf raised his head and sniffed the east wind. Then he turned to his right and the wind began to blow from the south, *nituka tua*[44]. Again, Wolf sniffed the air and repeated his actions to the west, *nituka tapai-yak init*[45], and finally to the north, *nituku*[46].

"Aieeeee!" he exclaimed. "I have found the source of this wonderful smell."

41   Fowler, *Anthropology of the Numa* 247.
42   Smith, *Ethnography of the Northern Utes* 280.
43   Smith, 268.
44   Smith, 268.
45   Smith, 268.
46   Smith, 268.

"Let us make a feast for *Itza*," smiled the Crane People. "Here, Little Brother, have some of this." Piñon soup, as thin as water, was poured from their pot into Coyote's sack. It ran through the sack and onto the ground. Coyote hung his head as he returned to his people with only a mud-caked sack to show for his efforts.

"My people, follow me!" Wolf called as he started through the Ice door. When the Crane People confronted him, he replied, "We only come to play *naipi*, the hand game, with you."

With that, Wolf spread a buffalo robe on the ground. He and his wife sat on one side and two old men from the Crane Nation sat opposite them. A long pole was placed across the center of the blanket and a man sat at each end of the pole beating it with a big stick. Wolf took a four-inch section of a deer leg bone marked in the center with a heavy paste of black pine pitch and hid it in his hand. His wife did the same with an identical bone. As the singing continued they fumbled with the bones trying to confuse their opponents. First, Wolf placed the fist of his left hand on top of the fist of his right and then reversed the procedure over and over. Finally, when he could see that Crane was wondering, *Did he drop the bone into his other hand?* Wolf and his wife crossed their arms, tucking their hands into their armpits.

At this, the music and singing changed to a different tempo and one Crane Elder pointed to Wolf's left hand.

"*Humph!*" growled Wolf, and he pulled up one of the foot-long willow sticks planted upright in the sand on Crane's side and placed it on a pile in front of him. Crane scowled and the music and the guessing continued. Finally, Crane correctly guessed which hand held the bone segment, triumphantly claimed possession of it, and the game began again.[47] All of Wolf's people and all of Crane's people gathered around them, laughing and shouting as the counters mounted in piles. Darkness fell around them, and still the music and the game continued.

Under the cover of this distraction, little mouse quietly scampered throughout Crane's camp. He sniffed Crane's buffalo robes, his hide boxes, and his fire pit. At last, he came to Crane's bow and inhaled deeply. *Aha! Piñon nuts!* Crane had carefully hollowed a section of the bow, stored the nuts, and securely wrapped the section with sinew. Mouse scampered off to tell Coyote and Coyote slunk through the camp and whispered in Wood Pecker's ear, "They are hidden in Crane's bow. Fly there and peck an opening."

When he had the nuts, Wood Pecker flew to the long pole in front of Wolf and began to peck at it in rhythm with the music. At this pre-arranged signal, Wolf and his wife rose from the game. Wolf led his people back to their own village in a long line. Coyote followed at the very end.

Crane stood watching their guests until they disappeared over the hillside then turned to his people saying, "Let us now have a feast of piñon nuts!" Grabbing his bow, he unstrung the sinew wrapping only to find an empty hole. "What is this? They have stolen our nuts! Come, follow me!" And with that he gave out a loud war whoop. Every man grabbed his weapons and ran to overtake the fleeing thieves. Coyote was the first they overtook and they clubbed him on the head, killing him. One by one, up the line of Wolf's people, they clubbed

---

47   This description of the Hand Game comes from Anne M. Smith *Ethnography of the Northern Utes*, 228-230. Frances Densmore also gives an account of this game and the accompanying songs in *Northern Ute Music* (Government Printing Office, 1922) 174 -179. Also, a description of the game comes from the author's own observation of the Hand Game as played by the Northern Ute at Garden of the Gods in 2005.

them dead until at last they came to Hawk who had hidden the piñon nuts in his leg.

"*Yewww!* This man stinks too much. He probably doesn't have them." And with that they turned around and went back home. When they were out of sight Coyote raised himself on one elbow and cautiously looked around. When he saw that there were no more enemies in sight he quickly passed from body to body bringing his people back to life. All of Wolf's people gathered at the Mountain and heatedly discussed what should be done with the piñon nuts.

At last Coyote spoke up, "I will chew the piñon nuts and mix them with water in my mouth and spurt them out over the ground around the mountain and they shall grow." And this is the origin of piñon trees around *Tiva Kaiv*, Piñon Nut Mountain.

WHAT CAN WE LEARN FROM "COYOTE OBTAINS PINE NUTS"?

It is intriguing and instructive to try to locate the Ute people at the time this story originated. There are a number of key elements, that, when taken together narrow the location of this story to the Four Corners area of Colorado, New Mexico, Utah, and Arizona. These elements include the following: the Crane People were nearby; there was an icy barrier; there were mountain sheep; the Utes were cooking in a pot; and eventually there was a mountain with piñon nuts.

First, where were the Crane People located? In 1776, Dominguez and Escalante made an epic journey from Santa Fe up into southwestern Colorado. Their detailed journal of this saga includes reference to a trail that runs along the base of Chimney Rock, as well as to a mountain range east of Pagosa Springs that their guides called La Sierra de la Grulla (The Mountains of the Cranes).[48] Today, we refer to this particular area as Wolf Creek Pass which lies adjacent to the migratory fly way used by thousands of Sandhill Cranes each year.

In this legend, it is said that Lightening Hawk smashed the ice barrier and made a doorway for the people. This second clue is a possible reference to Wolf Creek Pass. Ute people generally referred to a pass as a doorway, just as they refer to Ute Pass as the Doorway to the Red Earth Mountains (Puerto del Almagre) on the 1795 Spanish map.[49]

Representations of mountain sheep abound in the petroglyphs of the Four Corners area where they were abundant. In this legend, Coyote makes a soup out of

48   Ted J. Warner, editor, *The Dominguez-Escalante Journal* (Utah UP, 1995) 10, map 144-145.
49   Celinda Reynolds Kaelin, *American Indians of the Pikes Peak Region* (Arcadia Publishing, 2008) 76.

mountain sheep, giving us a third clue. Later, mouse finds the piñon nuts in a hollow section of a hunting bow that has been wrapped with sinew. The mountain sheep bow is one of the material culture markers of the Ute People. Ethnographer Anne Smith gives more details on the making of these bows.

> The horn bow was made of mountain sheep horn. The horn was warmed by placing it close to the fire. When it was softened by the heat, it was split and the two split pieces were spliced together, and the splice was wrapped with sinew. While still soft, the bow was shaped into a single curve. The horn bow was under three feet in length, shorter than the later wood bow. The grip and both ends were wrapped with buckskin. It was usually sinew-backed.[50]

Both of these references to mountain sheep would again seem to indicate that the actions described in this legend take place in the Four Corners area.

Our fourth clue as to location comes from the fact that coyote cooks his soup in a pot. The Four Corners area abounds in pottery, including that of the Anasazi. It is also the ancestral land of the Ute. It is not commonly known that the Ute People embraced aspects of Puebloan–Anasazi culture. However, ethnographer Frances Densmore interviewed a Northern Ute woman to this effect.

> Wiyu'ts, an aged [Ute] woman who recorded the first three of these songs, said that she learned them from her mother up in the canyon. When she was a little girl her mother sang them to her and told her of the time when the wolves [Utes] were people... Their dishes were made of sand and dirt. They made kettles of sand

---

50   Smith, *Ethnography of the Northern Utes* 108.

and dirt and boiled meat in them. They also made frying pans and plates. After they made these things they had a fire, and when the fire was red they put the dishes in the fire for a long time, which made them hard and strong.[51]

Archaeologists have also noted pottery found in western Colorado which is identified as Ute.

Brown ware pottery, finished by the paddle and anvil technique instead of the scraped technique employed by the pueblo groups to the south, each exhibits a conical base rather than round bottoms such as are common on pueblo pottery. From all appearances, this pottery is Shoshonean (i.e. Ute) production.[52]

Ethnographer Ann Smith's study of Ute culture contains a similar revelation.

[C]lay pots were used for boiling meat, sometimes with seed or yampa flour added. The pot was placed near the fire, and hot ashes were heaped around it. Sometimes hot stones were placed in with the food to make it boil faster.[53]

Finally, the Mesa Verde area, that borders the Southern Ute Reservation on the east and the Mountain Ute Reservation on the west, abounds in piñon trees.
The five clues place the location of this legend in the Four Corners area.

---

51   Densmore, *Northern Ute Music* 200-201.
52   Smith, *Ethnography of the Northern Utes* 88.
53   Smith, 87.

Origin of the Canyons of the Colorado [54]

A long time ago, a great chief among the Utes lost his beloved wife. He mourned day and night and would not be comforted. At last, one night he fell into a troubled sleep. He tossed and turned and toward morning had a powerful dream. *Ta-vwoats* (Rabbit, a powerful spirit) appeared to him.

"Your grandfathers see your tears and they have had pity on you. I will show you the way to the Spirit World where your wife now lives. You may see her and be assured that she is now happy and content. However, remember that you must leave your grieving once you have seen her."

With that, *Ta-vwoats* showed the chief the location of the underground passage, *Tu-wip pu-ru'-kwa po,* which led to the land of the dead, *Na-gun-tu-wip.*

In the morning, *Tavaci* (Chief) called his people together and told them of his dream and why he must leave them.

"My people, I have been shown something sacred, and now I must make my journey."

They loaded the sacred pipe, *cuuci,* with tobacco and passed it around the council so that each person could send his prayers for their chief's travels to the Spirit World. *Tavaci* then set out to the southwest and traveled for many days and nights until he came to the place he was shown in his dream. That night, as promised, *Ta-*

54   Fowler 66-69, 76-77.

vwoats appeared before him, beckoning him to follow. In the darkness, *Tavaci* saw an opening darker than the charcoal left from fire. As they entered the tunnel, *Tavaci* could no longer see *Ta-vwoats*. Instead he followed the sound of his footsteps. *Tu-wip pu-ru-kwa po*, the underground passage to the land of the dead, was a place to test the bravest warrior's heart. Strange beasts growled from the darkness and once or twice *Tavaci* stumbled into the deep track left by some unseen monster animal. *Tavaci* quickly ducked his head as the *whoosh* of giant wings fanned the air by his head. When he looked up it seemed that a great bird had landed on a boulder near the top of the passage scattering stones in a cascade down the side walls. At last they came out into the light.

"Follow me," *Ta-vwoats* instructed *Tavaci*, then took his magical ball and rolled it before them. It was a bright globe of fire and as it rolled it cut through the earth and the mountains and crushed all the rocks in its path. Soon the wind carried off the dust and the last rumblings of the boulders and *Tavaci* could see a clear trail running through the mountains. He and *Ta-vwoats* set off at a trot along the newly opened path, barely able to keep up with the burning ball of light. At last they came to a great chasm, *Pa-kup*, spanned by a bridge, *Na-gum-pa-sug*, to the Spirit World.

Only *Tavaci's* love for his departed wife gave him the courage to place his moccasins on *Na-gum-pa-sug*. The bridge was so narrow that he had space for only one foot in front of the other with the vast chasm of *Pa-kup* below ready to swallow him. Step by careful step he crossed to the other side, not daring to look down.

When he arrived, *Shin-au-am*, the Creator's beautiful daughter, greeted him there. She was dressed in soft white buckskin with fringes as long as a wolf's leg. Light glistened from her shiny black hair like sunshine on a raven. Her smile was warm and welcoming.

"Come with me," she said in a softly echoing voice. "You will find your wife among the dancers." She took his hand and they glided down into the valley of *Na-gun-tu-wip*, the land of the spirits of the dead. Laughter and music filled the air around them and they watched as the people danced and feasted. There was an abundance of game and fish and birds sang in every tree. People freely came and filled their bowls from the basket of pine nuts in the lodge but no matter how much they took the basket remained full. *Tavaci* watched these joyful people day and night as they passed by him in their finest regalia; still he

did not see his beloved wife. Patiently he waited another day and night. When he grew tired, *Shin-au-am* brought him meat and drink to refresh himself. "Don't worry, she will come." She assured him. After many days, *Tavaci's* wife finally appeared among the circling dancers.

"Husband," she cried, and fell into his arms. Weeping with joy, they held one another for several minutes before they could speak.

"My beloved, how I have missed you. Are you okay? Do they treat you well here?"

"*Aieeee!* Do you not see that there is always music

and laughter here? There is no sorrow or pain. There is always food with constant feasting and dancing. I am well but for missing you. But soon, my husband, you will join me here and we will be together. Your time is not yet, however."

"Yes, *Shin-au-am* has told me as much. I was only allowed here so that my heart would be at peace knowing you are safe and well cared for. I must return now, as I promised, but I will carry you in my heart." As soon as these words were out of his mouth, his wife and the beautiful valley turned to mist and dissolved into the air. Once again *Tavaci* was standing at the edge of the great chasm with *Ta-vwoats* beside him.

"My friend," *Ta-vwoats* voice was deep and firm. "You must never travel this trail again as long as you are alive. Now, you must grieve no more for your woman. You may tell your people of all you have seen in *Na-gun-tu-wip*, but no one must attempt to make this journey. For that reason, I am bringing these waters."

As he said this, there was a deafening roar like that of thunder as a great wall of water appeared. It raged into the gorge made by the ball of fire, and closed this trail to the spirit world to all who would try that path.

WHAT CAN WE LEARN FROM "ORIGINS OF THE CANYONS OF THE COLORADO"?

This legend is interesting from a geological as well as historical perspective. In much the same vein as "Rabbit Kills the Sun" (Chapter 2), this story possibly refers to the Clovis Comet. Geologically, the great flood referred to in this story could very well be a result of a comet. Historically, it seems to place the Ute at the Grand Canyon.

Although the Clovis Culture is the earliest in North America, it abruptly disappeared about 12,800 years ago. In over 50 archaeological sites related to this culture scientists have discovered "black mats" of dark organic deposits containing nanodiamonds which are signature traces left from a comet.[55] These sites are the latest and most compelling evidence that a comet was responsible for the demise of both the Clovis people and the mega fauna of the same time period.

As the earth's atmosphere destroyed this comet there was an enormous airburst – a ball of fire – over North America. At the time, vast areas of North America were covered by the Laurentide ice sheet which was over a thousand feet high and hundreds of miles wide. The airburst vaporized this ice sheet and the rush of melt water created a mega flood that rushed from the Colorado Plateau to the Gulf of Mexico. This flood is thought to have created the Grand Canyon and other dramatic landscapes in the American Southwest.[56]

Scientists tell us that the closest linguistic relatives of the Ute are the Southern Paiute and the Chemehuevi. Coincidently, their ancestral lands include the Grand Canyon and the lower Colorado River. Does this legend

55   Floyd Largent, "Mammoth Trumpet – The Clovis Comet," January 2008.
56   "Clovis Comet & North American Mass Extinction" www. SciForums.com, printed 1/2/2009

preserve the story of this life-changing geologic event?

Could the Ute Nation be descended from the Clovis culture? They are one of the few North American Indian nations that have no migration legend. They say that they were created here. Could this legend corroborate this claim?

The Flood [57]

A long time ago, the sea became angry. At first it moved back and forth, just a little. After a while, however, great waves began to build and rolled toward the land. They continued to grow and the cold, black waters churned violently. Finally, they attacked the land with all their fury.

When *Tov-wats* heard the roaring waters approach, he ran to warn the *Sunawiv* brothers, *Sunif* (Wolf) and his little brother *Yahowitz* (Coyote). *Tov-wats* was Rabbit Chief at this time. All of the people today come from him, they are his grandchildren

"Run! Run!" he cried in alarm. "The waters are angry and are attacking all over the land. We must run to the top of that mountain and we will be safe."

A thunderous roar filled the air and the angry waters licked at their heels as the three raced for their lives. They dodged around trees, jumped over rocks, and desperately clawed the sides of steep ravines, all the time climbing higher and higher. At last they found a steep trail along the edge of a mountain and raced upward, carefully placing one foot in front of the other on the narrow ledge while the waters churned and whirled in the canyon on their left. When they finally reached the summit of the mountain they fell exhausted onto the ground. Water dashed against the rocks all around them but couldn't reach the rocky pinnacle.

Tov-wats lay for a few more minutes then walked over to the thrashing waters, stooped down, and drank

---

57   Fowler, *Anthropology of the Numa* 75, 77-78.

deeply.

"Come on, the water is fine! You can drink. It cannot reach you now."

Wolf and Coyote watched Rabbit for a few minutes. Then, encouraged by his words, they carefully approached. Their race had made them quite thirsty. At that moment, a great wave rose and dashed itself at them.

"*Owuu! Owuu!*" they howled, and raced back to the safety of their boulder.

Tov-wats was angry now. "I think I will do something," he said, then pulled his bow and arrow from the heavily fringed quiver hanging from his left shoulder. He carefully slid the arrow onto the bowstring, pulled back, and sent the arrow into the heart of the waters. *Whoosh!* The water scattered into a million tiny drops, flew up into the sky, and fell in torrents of rain all over the world. Since that day, whenever the sea is angry, *Tov-wats* shoots an arrow and drives it back from the land. The waters flood up the side to the sky, and then fall back to the earth as rain. That is the lightening that you see. It is *Tov-wats* magic arrow.

Tov-wats, Sunif, and *Yahowitz* looked around them as the gentle rain began to fall. As far as they could see, every tree, every plant, every blade of grass had been

109

killed by the angry water. There was nothing to eat.

"*Owuu! Owuu!*" howled the brothers. "We have nothing to eat. We will die from our empty bellies!"

"Come with me, Grandsons." *Tov-wats* then led them on a winding path to a large, flat rock. He pointed to a small hole underneath. "Dig there, and see what you can find."

Rocks and dust flew up and around them as the brothers dug beneath the boulder. Their hunger drove them to dig and dig until at last they stopped to catch their breath. They looked at one another and then at the hole.

"*Tov-wats* has fooled us!" They snarled in disgust, and then they flung themselves on the ground under a tree.

"What are you doing? Why are you not digging where I showed you? Aren't you hungry?" *Tov-wats* chided the brothers for not following his instructions. They angrily responded.

"You have tricked us. There is no food here!"

"Watch, and I will show you something," *Tov-wats* replied, and then began to dig under the boulder. In a few minutes he disappeared down a hole. When Wolf and Coyote walked over to look, they were amazed to see a large chamber beneath the small opening. It was lined with stones and filled with every kind of seed. The hungry brothers ate and ate until their bellies could hold no more.

"Now that you have satisfied your hunger you must prepare the way for future generations. You must take these seeds and scatter them all over the land." *Sunif* and *Yahowitz* did as *Tov-wats* instructed. Today you can see all the plants and grasses and trees that came from the seeds in that hole under the boulder and were saved from the flood.

WHAT CAN WE LEARN FROM "THE FLOOD"?

Just as in the stories of "Rabbit Kills the Sun" and the "Origin of the Canyons of the Colorado," this story may also preserve the memory of the Clovis Comet. It is understandable that such a cataclysmic event would be commemorated with numerous stories. On the other hand, this story could simply be the result of deductive reasoning on the part of the Ute people. They undoubtedly found seashells from the great inland sea on mountain tops, and sought an explanation.

However, this story makes it a point that Rabbit drank from the flood waters. This would not be possible if they were the salty waters of the inland ocean. Also, the melting of the Laurentide ice sheet would have provided fresh, drinkable, water. A second important point is that the flood came on quite suddenly and Rabbit and the *Sunawiv* brothers had to run for their lives. This again would indicate that the story refers to the Laurentide ice sheet rather than a pre-existing ocean.

Another interesting insight that this story provides is the use of food caches or cists. Powell had this to say concerning the Ute people and these caches.

A cache is a hiding or storing away of any articles of value which may be used at some future time. When the season for gathering seeds is passed many of the baskets used for this purpose are thus placed away to be ready for next year, but stores of food are the principal objects thus temporarily put away. I have observed two methods of making caches; one was to dig a hole in the ground, and in its place the articles to be preserved. It was then covered with stones, and sand raked over the top. Then fire is built over this and kept up perhaps for two or three days which serves a double purpose first to hide all evidences that might otherwise have appeared to indicate the position of the cache, to persons who might be passing, and second, which is the principal cause as asserted by the Utes, to destroy the odor by which wolves or other animals might be attracted to the spot.

Many caches are made in caves and crevices, which are everywhere to be found in this region of canons and cliffs, the seeds or other articles being placed in baskets or sacks, and sometimes covered with bast of cedar, and over the whole a huge pile of stones is placed.

A cache in the rocks or cave is called To-go'-i. A cache in the ground I called U-rai'-go-i.[58]

Use of these caches or cists by the Ute people is another significant cultural link to the Anasazi. At the 1991 Anasazi Symposium at Mesa Verde National Park, Ralph J Hartley presented research on the Anasazi which included the documentation on their use of cists. He describes a cist (food cache) as being a "depression dug into floor of shelters and lined with rock on bottom and side; covered with timbers and thatch and used for storage of food and non-food materials; also includes 'hardpan' or 'earthen' cists not lined with rock."[59]

Archaeologists Muench and Pike also report on the use of these cists by the Anasazi.

The earliest Anasazi were the Basket Makers...[who had] elaborate slab-lined cists. The cists were carefully constructed circular holes dug in the loose fill of the caves, sometimes six feet in diameter and two feet deep, and lined with flat rocks fitted to prevent the

---

58   Fowler, *Anthropology of the Numa* 49.
59   Ralph J. Hartley, "Rockshelters and Rock Art: An Assessment of Site Use." *Proceedings of the Anasazi Symposium* 1991 (Mesa Verde Museum Association, Inc., 1991) 165-177.

sides from collapsing. Food, seed corn, and household items were apparently stored in them and carefully covered.[60]

Florence Lister's research illustrates Anasazi cists that bear remarkable similarity to the Ute caches recorded by Powell.

The cone-shaped pits were gouged by digging sticks about three feet down into a deep bank of clay, which formed the feature walls. The floors had diameters of three to nine feet and were flat. Pit mouths were restricted and had been sealed with thin, large, worked sandstone slabs that, after abandonment, had slumped into the interior fill. All but one of the pits had been burned prior to being used, which hardened the clay walls to an imperviousness sufficient to thwart rodent and insect activity and moisture seepage. The sandstone covers showed no comparable fire reddening.[61]

Further cultural homogeneity of these cists is provided by ethnographer Ann Smith who uses a similar description from her Ute informants.

Places where snow was not apt to be too heavy were selected for caches. Holes were dug under cliff overhangs, and these pits were lined with bark. ..The sacks were then covered with bark, grass and rocks, then dirt and more rocks... When the pit was adequately covered, a fire was built on top to destroy

60   David Muench and Donald G. Pike, *Anasazi: Ancient People of the Rock* (American West Publishing Co., 1974) 45.
61   Florence C. Lister *In the Shadow of the Rocks: Archaeology of the Chimney Rock District in Southern Colorado* (The Herald Press, 1997) 71.

evidence that a pit had been dug.[62]

In Florissant, Colorado, there are some excellent examples of Ute *To-go'-i* on Fortification Hill. Arthur Lakes documented these caches when he visited Florissant in 1877, describing them as "remarkable funnel like holes in portions of the massive lava and smooth and circular as a funnel about a foot in diameter..."[63]

However, an early history of the Colorado Midland Railroad mistakenly identifies at least one these cists as being used to store water.

Fortification Hill is the name of a hill within the town limits, where it is supposed the [Utes] fought bloody and desperate battles years ago. All over the hill are breastworks built of rocks, just as the Indians left them, and on the side in a large rock is what has been named The Mortise. This is a deep, smooth hole cut into solid rock. It is about 18 inches in diameter and 3 feet deep.[64]

There are at least six of these cists on Fortification Hill, and several of them still have their finely shaped, round stone covers or lids.[65]

In conclusion, this particular legend seems to make two important points. It corroborates the earlier stories commemorating the Clovis Comet and it provides a link between Anasazi and Ute use of cists or food caches.

---

62   Smith, *Ethnography of the Northern Utes* 67.
63   Michael F. Kohl and John S. McIntosh, editors,. *Discovering Dinosaurs in the Old West – The Field Journals of Arthur Lakes* (Smithsonian Institution Press, 1997) 49.
64   Leo Kimmett, *Florissant, Colorado* (Master Printers, 1980) 70.
65   Kaelin, *Pikes Peak Backcountry* 11.

Origins of the People [66]

Long time ago, when the earth was young, all things in this world could speak. Animals could speak, the water could speak, the skies, the stars, the four-leggeds and those with wings, even the little bugs. "We shall make this world the way that it will be comfortable for those who are going to live here, the Indian people. He will then take care of it in the right way because the instructions will come from us." Those are the words of wisdom from the animals and all things around him. Thus are the stories that I'm going to tell.

The coyote will be the main character and his older brother the wolf. *Sunif,* Older Brother (Wolf), and *Yahowitz* (Coyote) lived in a *carniv,* a cloud tipi, on top of Pikes Peak. Many, many moons ago, to the south, a journey was to be made throughout the world into the high countries of this world. *Sunif* wanted to put the people here and there, so he made a little bag and this he will pack on his back and as he moves to the north he will distribute these little people throughout the world. All will be placed in the right place, on their own land, so they will not fight one another. He did not tell anyone what he was doing. But his brother, *Yahowitz,* was a curious animal. In Indian stories he was a trickster. He was curious. And he murmured, "*Ahat iya aqay*?" What is he doing? The Older Brother was breaking these small twigs to small size and putting them in a bag. But the Younger brother watched without getting too close.

---

66   As told by Clifford Duncan, 5/7/1998, author's collection.

Now the older brother *Sunif* decided to take a walk and when he was gone curiosity got the best of his younger brother *Yohowitz*. In the bag he could hear people talking. There's music going on in the bag. He'd listen real carefully and he would say, "*Niahook?*" What's it

saying, what is in there? So he took his flint knife and he cut a little hole on the side of the bag. In the meantime, his older brother is gone but he knew that he's getting close again. And when he looked in through the hole the people saw him. There were people in there. The sticks had turned into people. And some jumped out and about that time the older brother came back again. Not knowing what had taken place he put the bag on his back. And *Sunif* moved on his journey. As he was going along he'd be singing a song. Like the heartbeat of the earth, the drums would be going and he'd be singing to that.

Every once in while he would stop and reach in the bag and put some people down on the earth and say, "You will live here." But as he went on he noticed that the bag was getting lighter and he knew that he didn't put that many people out. Finally, when he got to the high place *waaaay* up in the mountains, he knew what was going on. There was a hole in the bag and all the people had jumped out. But the Ute and Hopi were still in there. He left them in there until they were fully ripe. He placed the Hopi on their land. Then he talked to the last of them that were ripe. They were now fully human.

"You my people, you my children, I'm going to put you over here. You will be called the *Yutica, Yuta*, the Ute. You will live in these mountains for these shining mountains will be your home. From here you will see across the plains to the east and to the north and to the west and to the south."

And that's how the distribution was made and how the Utes were placed on the mountains. Then they dropped off all the people that were supposed to have been placed around and those are the little tribes here and there scattered to the south and to the west, and that's where we came from.

WHAT CAN WE LEARN FROM "ORIGINS OF THE PEOPLE"?

This legend is important for two of its historic aspects. It underscores the close identity of the Ute with their ancestral lands and it also underscores that the Ute and the Hopi were one nation until they split apart in the 1300s.

As noted in the introduction, a medicine wheel was built in the center of every Ute village. These medicine wheels varied in size but not design. Traditionally, they consisted of a circle surrounding a cross with all sides the same length. At the center was a large "heartstone," where offerings were made to Mother Earth.[67] This medicine wheel became like an umbilical cord, deeply connecting the Ute people to the earth.

Powell reported that this geo-identity was profound among the Ute people.

> An Indian will never ask to what nation or tribe or body of people another Indian belongs but to 'what land do you belong and how are you land named?'... His national pride and patriotism, his peace with other tribes, his home and livelihood for his family, all his interests, everything that is dear to him is associated with his country.[68]

A good example of this "land naming" is the band of Ute Indians that originated at Pikes Peak. The Ute name for Pikes Peak, *Tava* (Sun), was incorporated into the band name, *Tabeguache*, the People of Sun Mountain. When this band was relocated to the western slope after the Treaty of 1868, they became known as the *Uncompahgre*, a distortion of the word *aka-paa-garu-ri*, place of the red

---

67   Author Interview, Clifford Duncan 3/10/1998.
68   Fowler, *Anthropology of the Numa* 38.

water sitting. At least half a dozen medicine wheels still mark the sites of Ute villages on the slopes of Pikes Peak massif.

As this legend makes clear, the Ute people felt that Creator had placed each race of people on the earth in their designated area. Powell further clarifies the importance attached to this land placement.

> The whole region of country occupied by these tribes...is divided into districts with lines separating them, well defined, usually by natural objects and to each of such districts there belongs a tribe [band] of Indians [Ute] who take the name of the land and the Indians are fixed to this land... To go elsewhere to obtain a subsistence they must join and become recognized as a member of another tribe.[69]

This vital issue of land sovereignty can probably be best understood from the point of view of the hunter-gatherer. In order to feed their people it was necessary to develop a deep knowledge of the land and the resources which it could provide, and in which seasons these resources were available. For example, if elk were best hunted in the fall at a certain mountain, then each year the band would adjourn to that mountain for hunting. However, if another band had encroached on this hunting area, the elk would have left and your band would be at risk of starvation. Again, Powell expands our understanding of this issue from his interviews with the people.

> One of the most important subjects discussed in the Council is the matter of the route of travel for the season. As it often involves the matter of right of convenience of other tribes [bands], the chief himself, or some of the leading men, are usually sent to consult

69 Fowler, *Anthropology of the Numa* 38.

with neighboring tribes [bands] concerning their proposed travels so that there will be no interference on the hunting grounds...Tribes [bands] are very tenacious in clinging to their rights over such places, and very jealous of the encroachments of other [bands].[70]

The journals that Dominguez and Escalante kept in 1776 also reference the use of natural boundaries to mark Native American territory. For example, they report that the northern section of the Rio Grande River separates the Navajo and Ute nations. Specifically, they report that the Rio de Las Paraliticas (the Dolores River, near Durango, Colorado) separates the lands of the Tabeguache (Northern) and the Moache (Southern) Utes.[71]

When we look at the Ute people through the dual lenses of the historical records and this legend, we can see that they had a deep spiritual and practical connection with the earth. They were not simply gypsies that harvested the land and moved on.

The Shin-Au-Av Brothers Discuss

70   Fowler, *Anthropology of the Numa* 39.
71   Warner, *The Dominguez-Escalate Journal* 11, 21.

Matters of Importance to the People[72]

A long time ago, the *Shin-au-av* brothers (Wolf and Coyote) met on top of a high mountain to discuss the destiny of the Ute Nation.

"My Brother," said *Yahowitz* (Coyote). "How will these people get their food? How will they feed themselves? We need to make a good plan for them. Last night I thought about this all night long. Still, I couldn't see what would be best for them. So this morning I got up before the sun and climbed to the top of this mountain. I sat here and thought and thought about this problem."

Sunif (Wolf) yawned and stretched. "Well, tell me. What did you decide?"

"Listen to your younger brother," *Yahowitz* gently chided. "I can tell you a good plan. *Tu-wap* (piñon pine) grows all around us and its nuts are sweet. *Us* (yucca) has fruit that is very rich, and apple of the *mana-vi* (cactus) is full of juice. Down below the mountains, the *kupu* (sunflowers) grow and their seeds give many delicious seeds. The people can gather all of these foods and then store them for times of need. They can dig a hole and place them in the ground or they can hide them in the rocks. That way whenever they come back to a place they will have plenty to eat. Even when they return a second or third time, this food will be there for them. This way they will never be hungry and will always have enough to eat without working."

---

72   Fowler, *Anthropology of the Numa* 80-81.
Also, Unitah-Ouray Tribe 7.

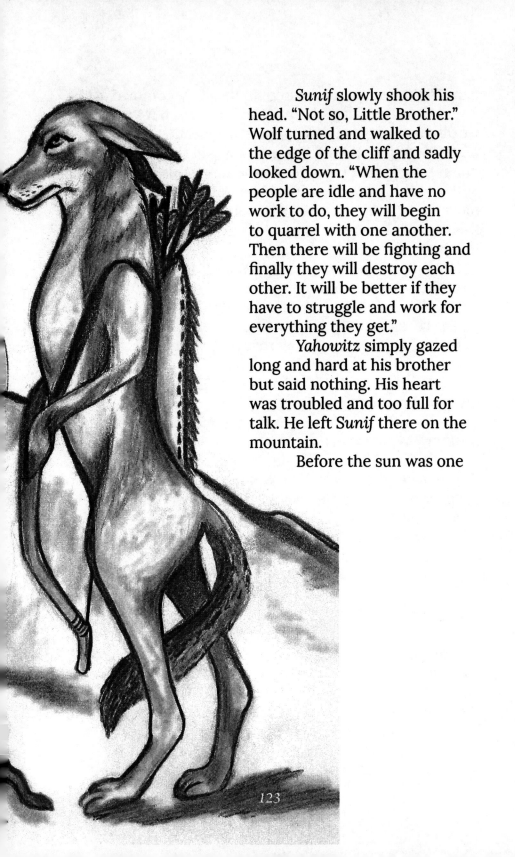

Sunif slowly shook his head. "Not so, Little Brother." Wolf turned and walked to the edge of the cliff and sadly looked down. "When the people are idle and have no work to do, they will begin to quarrel with one another. Then there will be fighting and finally they will destroy each other. It will be better if they have to struggle and work for everything they get."

Yahowitz simply gazed long and hard at his brother but said nothing. His heart was troubled and too full for talk. He left Sunif there on the mountain.

Before the sun was one

hand high, *Yahowitz* accosted *Sunif* the next morning.

"Brother, it was hard for me to hear, but your words yesterday were very wise. We must let the Ute people work for their food. But how will they get their honey-dew? Last night I thought about this all night long. Still, I couldn't see what would be best for them. So this morning I got up before the sun and climbed to the top of this mountain. I sat here and thought and thought about this problem."

Yahowitz rubbed his chin thoughtfully and looked intently at *Sunif* before continuing.

"Brother, we can let the honey-dew fall like snow on the rocks and the women can go early in the morning to gather it. They can get all that they want, and they will be glad."

Sunif shook his head again. "This will not be good, my little brother."

Surprised, *Yahowitz*, spun around to face his brother. "What is this you say?"

"If the Utes have so much and it is so easy to get, they will come to think of it as dung. What we give them for pleasure will just be wasted. Instead, we shall cause it to fall in small drops on the reeds. Then they can gather these and lick the dew from the stems, relishing each drop. When it is so scarce and difficult to get, it will taste much sweeter and they will value it more highly."

Yahowitz hung his head in sorrow and slowly walked away.

On the following morning, coyote and wolf again met on the mountain top to continue their deliberations. Once more, *Yahowitz* began the discussion.

"My brother, your words are wise. We shall have the women work hard to gather the honey-dew. They will beat the reeds with flails to get this precious sweetness."

Coyote sat quietly for a few moments before continuing, for this next issue was of great importance.

When his thoughts were collected, he again addressed wolf.

"Older Brother, when a man or a woman, or a boy, or a girl, or a little one dies, where shall they go? Last night I thought about this all night long, still, I couldn't see what would be best for the people. So this morning I got up before the sun and climbed to the top of this mountain. I sat here and thought and thought about this problem. This is what we should do. When a man dies, let us send him back when the morning comes. Then his family and friends will be very happy."

"Not so," *Sunif* disagreed. "The dead will return no more."

Coyote's shoulders slumped and he turned away from his brother. Without saying a word he slowly walked back down the mountain.

Not long afterward, the younger *Shin-au-av* was walking among the pine trees when he saw *Sunif's* son at play. He took his bow from his back, deftly nocked an arrow, and shot the little boy. He said nothing to his brother when he returned home. As darkness shrouded the village, *Sunif* went to hunt for his missing child. After several days of searching, he came upon the body of the dead boy.

"My brother, you made the law that the dead should return no more. Now you know how this feels for yourself. I am glad that you were the first to suffer."

At these words, *Sunif* realized that *Yahowitz* had killed his son, and his jaw set in anger. As his rage grew and grew, the earth began to shake and deep groans came from her center. Darkness fell and terrible storms raged around the brothers while thunder rolled through the clouds and lightening flashed. Coyote fled to his father, *Tavweatch* (First Rabbit), and begged him to protect him.

WHAT CAN WE LEARN FROM "THE SHIN-AU-AV BROTHERS DISCUSS MATTERS OF IMPORTANCE TO THE PEOPLE"?

This legend raises several key points that bear further discussion. First, we have yet another allusion to the origins of the Ute people, and secondly we seem to have further corroboration of legend as oral history.

Sunif (Wolf) and *Tavweatch* (Rabbit) are two of the principal deities in the Ute hierarchy. But why is Rabbit so important? Perhaps we can find a clue in the very word "Ute." The Ute name is derived from Shoshone who "called the Ute 'Tsiuta' which means 'Rabbit Hunters.'"[73] Spanish later corrupted this to "Yuta," and Mountain Men further corrupted it to "Yutaws." Rabbit was a vital resource of food and clothing for the early Ute and so assumes a mythological role.

If you will remember from Chapter 2, it was *Tavweatch* who killed the sun. Powell further explains First Rabbit's relationship with wolf and coyote:

> Tov-wots is sometimes said to be the father of the Shin-au-av brothers. "When the sun is drawing water they say ta-vwoats [sic] has shot an arrow into the sea." [MS 1795, no11] When they observe lightning and hear thunder in the heavens they say Tov-wots is shooting at the clouds to make them rain. When the sun is drawing water they say Tov-wots is shooting in the sea.[74]

(I am sure you have noticed that there are several different spellings of Rabbit's name including *Tavweatch*, *Tov-wots*, and *Ta-vwoats* which when verbalized, sound

---

73   Robert Emmitt, "Indians in Colorado," *Denver Westerners Brand Book*, Vol XXX-XXXI 319.
74   Fowler MS 794-a, no. 29.

quite similar and explain the variations in spelling. This is common with all of the Ute words and names.)

This discussion, of course, also brings us to the question of Wolf's importance in mythology. Clifford, as noted in the introduction, explained it to me this way.

> Great Spirit, the Creator, is everywhere and in everything. He/She is always present. When Creator wanted to take on physical form, He/She used the form of Wolf. That's why Wolf represents Creator in our stories.
>
> Wolf always meant life for the people. Whenever the People heard Wolf's voice, they knew that the buffalo or the elk or the deer were nearby. Wolf's voice let them know that they would have food to eat, animal hides for clothes, shelter, and robes to keep them warm. When an enemy was near, Wolf always warned the People. Wolf was life. That is why Creator took on the form of wolf.[75]

Unfortunately, Powell's informants weren't as fluent in English as Clifford. This difficulty in communications is probably why Powell erroneously concluded that the Ute were zootheists and savages. This concept that I call "Unitheism" was most difficult for me to grasp when Clifford and I first began working together. He had to clarify over and over to me that Creator was energy, not an old man with a beard, and that Creator's energy pervaded everything. I think that most of us raised in traditional Judeo-Christian religions struggle to understand Creator as Energy rather than Person. But it is brilliant theology! Modern physics finally teaches us this ancient concept when it reveals that on a sub-atomic level, *everything* is simply energy.

As for the second aspect, we are again reminded

---

75   Author Interview, Clifford Duncan 3/10/1998.

that legend is truly oral history. Just as some of the earlier legends relate to actual historic events such as the Clovis Comet, so does this one. Powell's informants insisted that this particular legend related to the actual creation of several geographic points.

This quarrel is located on the Kai-bab Plateau and at the Cave Lakes near Kanab, Utah, which are said   to have originated during the storm. The two points are about thirty-five miles apart and how they connect them I cannot understand. The Indians appear to discover no discrepancy and yet at one time these conversations appear to be on the plateau and at another by the side of the lakes, and then again these lakes are made during the storm which ensued.

I first heard the story told by the Indians of White River in Colorado 400 miles away from where the scene is located and afterwards heard the Indians on the Kaibab Plateau tell it in substance in the same way.[76]

This legend, then, is a wonderful example of the historical and cultural significance of these stories.

---

76   Fowler MS 1795, 80.

The Story of the Moon[77]

The *Shin-au-av* brothers were sleeping under a tree but their slumbers were curiously disturbed.

Sunif sleepily brushed his hand over his head. "Go away!" he commanded. Still, whatever was moving on his head persisted. "I said, go away!" he angrily demanded and rolled onto his other side. Still, the annoying touch persisted so he jumped to his feet and stalked over to the sleeping *Yahowitz*.

"Little Brother, what is this trick that you play with me while I try to sleep?"

"What are you talking about? Let me sleep." Coyote pulled his blanket over his head. Then he felt something strange on his head, touching it all over. "Why do you torment me, I told you I did nothing to you." As he swatted at his head, he heard a deep buzzing. He slowly rubbed the sleep from his eyes and sat up to confront his older brother. Before his angry words could leave his mouth, however, he began to howl in laughter.

"*Aieeee*! What have you done? You look like the eagle with the bald head!"

Sunif ran his hand over the top of his head but all he felt were the short, wiry bristles where his long, silken hair had once been.

Once he realized what had happened, he lunged at coyote. "I'll teach you to cut my hair!"

Yahowitz held his stomach and continued to howl, falling to the ground in a spasm of laughter as his brother

---

77   Fowler, *Anthropology of the Numa* 81.
Unitah-Ouray Ute Tribe 88.

pounced on him. They rolled among the pine needles for several minutes, coyote howling in merriment while wolf pounded him with his fists. When they finally stood again, *Sunif* began to laugh, pointing at his younger brother's bald head.

"*Aieeee!* You are also bald!" Now it was his turn to howl with laughter.

"What are you talking about? I haven't cut my hair!" However, as coyote rubbed the top of his head he also felt short, wiry bristles where his hair had been. "Who has done this thing to us?"

Buzzzzzz, buzzzzzz, buzzzzzz came the answer as members of the Fly Nation danced around their heads.

"Who are these little people? Why have they cut our hair? Let us follow them to their village and find out what we can about them."

The *Shin-au-av* brothers panted loudly as they scrambled up the hillside, following the buzzing war cry of the flies through the dark night. Their path wasn't easy to trace, for they zigzagged in a ragged flight up and down hills, over boulders and streams, re-crossing several meadows. Finally they drew close to a thicket of pines where the buzzing sounded like one loud hiss of steam. Cautiously, the brothers peered from behind a fallen tree.

"What is that strange person?" *Yahowitz* asked. "All I can see is a pale blue light, and the flies seem to be placing our hair on it."

"Watch what I will do!" *Sunif* jumped from cover and swinging his tomahawk he dashed at the mysterious being while screaming his war cry, "*Waaagh!*" His brother followed close behind, and ran up just as *Sunif's* tomahawk landed on the strange being. With a loud thump the round head severed from the body and then began to float into the sky. It slowly wafted over the treetops until it was two hands above the place where the sun rose. Then it slowed and seemed to hang still.

"Older Brother, he has taken our hair! See how it falls over one side of his face?"

Both brothers sat on the ground and craned their necks at this strange thief. When they realized they would never recover their long, silken hair, they commenced a sad lament. "*Ou, ou, oiuuuu oiuuuu oiuuuu!!*"

WHAT CAN WE LEARN FROM "THE STORY OF THE MOON"?

This legend is a charming example of the rich imagery and playfulness of Ute storytelling. Who hasn't felt as if horseflies were using tiny knives when they bite? Now when I see the different phases of the Moon I imagine her long, silky hair falling over a part of her face. And, how amusing to think of Wolf and Coyote racing across the land with their long, silky hair trailing in the grass – before the flies cut it. The genius of these stories comes from the indelible images they evoke and from the illogical pairing of disparate factors. These are much like the "koans" of the Buddhist teachers, effectively placing a "great doubt" which fully engages the mind of the student.

As with so many of these legends, we also find clues to the origin and history of the Ute Nation. Earlier, I noted links with Mesoamerica and here again we find echoes of an early Mayan connection, specifically the *Popol Vuh*. In Chapter 1, the Sacred Twins (*So-kus Wai-un-ats*) were introduced, and now, just as the twins are beheaded by the Lords of Xibalba in the Mayan text, Wolf and Coyote also behead a strange being. When the Sacred Twin's severed heads rise into the sky they become the sun and the moon, just as the severed head in this story becomes the moon.[78]

These connections to the Mayan's *Popol Vuh* become even more logical when we remember that the Ute and the Mayan are linked linguistically. In Chapter 1, I noted that the Ute language is of the Uto-Aztecan family. What is less well known, however, is that when the Aztecs conquered the Toltecs they also adopted their culture and language.[79]

Sahagun's informants [Aztec] traced the origins of

78   Adrian Recinos, translator, *Popol Vuh* (Oklahoma UP) 163.
79   Leon-Portilla, *Fifteen Poets of the Aztec* 61. Miller 9-10.

their culture back to the 'golden age' of the Toltecs, a time when everything was good and beautiful. The word *Toltecayotl* had come to signify for them the sum total of all the arts and ideals inherited from the Toltecs.[80]

This high esteem for all things Toltec also manifested in the Aztec language "The Aztecs spoke Nahuatl, which was also the language of the Toltecs and several other cultures of ancient Mexico..."[81]

Therefore, Aztec, Toltec, and Maya are part of the same Macro-Penutlan language phylum.[82] Of course, other aspects of the culture were bound to manifest along with the language.

How and when did the Aztec-speaking people first arrive in North America? Most experts agree that the language undoubtedly arrived with corn.

Second, corn was introduced from Mexico [2000 B.C. to 500 B.C.] ...From excavations at Bat Cave in west-central New Mexico, we know that a small-cobbed popcorn, called chapalote was being cultivated there by approximately 1500 B.C. [Bat Cave was a 3-day walk from the San Juan basin][83]

The immigrations and migrations from the south were both sporadic (family, friends, religious groups) and periodic (traders, *pocheteca*), and continued for hundreds of years, just as we find people from the south coming into North America following family and looking for opportunity today.

---

80   Leon-Portilla, *Fifteen Poets of the Aztec* 167.
81   Holmer, *Aztec Book of Destiny* 3.
82   Leon-Portilla, *Fifteen Poets of the Aztec*, pxix -xx. John R. Swanton, *The Indian Tribes of North America* (Smithsonian Institution Press, 1969) 612.
83   David E. Stuart, *Anasazi America* (New Mexico UP, 2000) 35.

Wolf and Stone Shirt Have a Fight on the Mountain [84]

After *Sunif* and *Yahowitz* quarreled about the matters of food and death for the Ute People, *Tav-weatch* (First Rabbit) gave Coyote a man called *Tum-pwi-nai-ro-gwi-nump* (He Who Wears the Stone Shirt) as his champion to fight his battles.

Stone Shirt received his name because of the shirt, *Tum-pin-tog*, that he wore. No weapon could penetrate it. *Tav-weatch* also gave Stone Shirt a potent watchman, <u>*Tau-shants* (</u>Antelope of Many Eyes). Antelope had two

84 Fowler, *Anthropology of the Numa* 81-82. Uintah-Ouray Ute Tribe 8.

eyes in his head, one on each shoulder, one on each side of his rump, and two in his tail. He could see everywhere and everything.

Sunif was still angry with *Yahowitz* and wandered the land seeking to revenge himself on his younger brother for the death of his son. Fortunately for Coyote, Stone Shirt always received advance warning from Antelope about the approach of Wolf.

Antelope always traveled along a ridge, parallel to whatever trail *Sunif* took. He slept on the ridge but with each dawn he made certain that *Sunif* was gone. Once assured, he sang his scout's song, "Hi *yeah!* Hi *yeah!* No one is near!"[85]

Unfortunately, there came a time when the brothers and their people happened to be encamped on the opposite sides of the same mountain. Stone Shirt and Antelope went to the summit to stand guard.

One night while Stone Shirt slept, Antelope spied movement in *Sunif's* camp. Antelope watched intently as *Sunif* crept from his lodge and dashed to a nearby boulder. He waited for a few moments before slinking across the open meadow to the stone field leading to the summit. Slowly, boulder by boulder, he ran then sheltered, then ran again, gradually gaining the mountain top.

"Stone Shirt! Wake up!" Antelope urgently awakened the champion. "*Sunif* is almost upon us!"

"Watch what I will do!" Stone Shirt said as he jumped to his feet and prepared for battle just as *Sunif* crested the ridge. *Sunif* had his arrow nocked and sent it flying into Stone Shirt but it could not penetrate his armor and fell harmlessly to the ground. Stone Shirt's arrows wounded *Sunif* several times throughout the battle. However, his stone shirt made him invincible. *Sunif* and Stone Shirt fought this way until the sun was directly

---

85   Densmore, *Northern Ute Music* 150.

overhead, then Stone Shirt killed *Sunif*.

Stone Shirt and Antelope jubilantly returned to coyote's camp below.

Coyote's people were thrilled with their victory and began dancing the war dance and singing the war song.

Stone Shirt and Antelope were wildly excited as they danced about the fire, whooping and singing. They then cautioned their warriors. "Now, now run to your horses because our young men may be killed. If we go into the enemy's tents our scalps may be taken."[86]

In the midst of this revelry, Rabbit suddenly appeared, also warning them.

"Do not be so foolish! The enemy will rise again! Stop your dancing and singing and prepare yourselves for war!"

At once, the drumming and singing stopped and Coyote's people slowly wandered back to their lodges. Rabbit's stern warning sobered Stone Shirt and Antelope, and they returned to the mountain top to keep vigil.

Just before dawn Antelope again saw Wolf creeping up to their mountain lookout.

"Stone Shirt! Grab your spear! *Sunif* is about to attack you with his!"

These words were barely out of Antelope's mouth when Wolf lunged at Stone Shirt with his spear. Stone Shirt quickly dodged to the side and the sharp point simply bounced off his impenetrable shirt. As he regained his balance he thrust his spear into Wolf's leg and then retreated a few steps to regain striking distance. Wolf lunged at him again, but with the same result. Sun rose higher and higher in the sky while the two warriors fought. When Sun was directly overhead Stone Shirt dealt a fatal blow and Wolf fell to the ground.

Victorious, Stone Shirt and Antelope returned to Coyote's camp with the good news. Once more Rabbit

---

86   Densmore, *Northern Ute Music* 151.

interrupted their war dance.

"Do not be so foolish!" said Rabbit. "The enemy will rise again! Stop your dancing and singing and prepare yourselves for war!"

The following day, at exactly the same time and in exactly the same way, Antelope discovered Wolf returning for combat. Stone Shirt was prepared and met his opponent with a loud war whoop. This time they did battle with knives. They fought until noon, just as they had on the two previous days, then Wolf fell to the ground with Stone Shirt's knife in his heart.

When they returned to Coyote's camp for the war dance, *Tav-woatch* again appeared and chided them. When they returned to their post on the summit Antelope laid down and slept, exhausted from his three days of constant vigilance. Without his friend to warn him, Stone Shirt was still snoring when Wolf arrived to do battle and he was killed immediately.

Wolf called to his warriors waiting below and they streamed over the mountain and into Coyote's camp below, slaughtering nearly everyone. Coyote and some of his people escaped but he never rallied his warriors to battle Wolf again.

WHAT CAN WE LEARN FROM "WOLF AND STONE SHIRT HAVE A FIGHT ON THE MOUNTAIN"?

This legend raises several interesting points about the Ute people and their attitude toward death. Reincarnation is an integral part of their belief system, and their burial practices provide evidence of this. What the archaeological record is missing speaks volumes about the Ute and their antecedents. Archaeologist Joel Janetski illustrates this point in his study.

> A review of the known archaeological literature on [Ute] burials following the ethnographic pattern reveals that all date to the post-horse period and, when diagnostics are present, none can be shown to be older than the 1800s...It could suggest that burial patterns shifted in the historic period for reasons not yet understood.[87]

Many times in this volume I point to the connection of the Ute and the Toltec-Mayans. It is highly probable, then, that the lack of Ute burials prior to Spanish contact is another of these links. This particular legend emphasizes Wolf's ability to return to life again and again, and it is evocative of the Sacred Twins' similar ability in the *Popol Vuh*. In fact, one segment in particular might explain the absence of Ute burials prior to the horse and Spanish influence. Knowing that the Lords of Xibabla are going to kill them, the Twins give the following instructions:

> ...then it would be well to crush [our] bones on a grinding stone, as corn meal is ground; let each one be ground [separately]; throw [the powdered bones] into

---

87   Madsen, *Across the West* 174.

the river immediately...[88]

...But the bones did not go very far, for settling themselves down at once on the bottom of the river, they were changed back into handsome boys.[89]

Did the Ute people also follow this tradition so that their loved ones might reincarnate more quickly? If so, this would explain the lack of pre-conquest Ute burials. It might also explain one of the great mysteries of the Anasazi – a similar lack of burials.[90] If we factor in the Aztec-Toltec influence we are able get a better understanding of Anasazi identity. In Aztec-Toltec tradition there were separate rituals for the burial of warriors as opposed to other members of society.

Warriors were cremated, but women who died in childbirth were buried at sunset in the courtyard of the Temple...

Tlaloc, the god of rain and water, ruled over Tlalocan, the Southern Paradise. To his domain went the souls of those who had committed suicide, been struck by lightning, had drowned, or died of leprosy, rheumatism, or dropsy, the diseases associated with Tlaloc. The bodies were not cremated but were buried...

People who died of old age, or from a cause which did not qualify them for admittance to a paradise... were cremated.[91]

---

88   Recinos, *Popol Vuh* 154.

89   Recinos, *Popol Vuh* 155.

90   Robert H. and Florence C. Lister, *Chaco Canyon: Archaeology & Archaeologists* (New Mexico UP, 1981) 199-200.

91   Warwick Bray, *Everyday Life of the Aztecs* (Dorset Press, 1968) 70-73.

Does this perhaps explain why the ceremonial buildings at Chaco Canyon hold the most burials? Is this why many of the bones found among Anasazi ruins have cut marks and appear to have been burned or cooked? Until we factor in the spirituality of these ancient peoples we will not understand their archaeology.

The First Child Born [92]

O ne day, the *Shin-au-av* brothers were resting under a large pine tree.

"Someday we shall die and be no more. I would like to live forever!" complained the younger brother.

"Why do you talk like this? Why do you not think of the good things of today? The sun is warm, our bellies are full. We can see across this beautiful valley," chided his older brother as he sat up.

"But what a lonesome world this will be with no one left to walk it. What a pity that the world with all its good things will be wasted."

As they talked, their voices were suddenly silenced by the singing of the Goose Nation as they passed overhead. *Yahowitz* had never seen these people before and was filled with wonder.

"Aieee!" *Yahowitz* cried as he jumped to his feet. "See how high they can travel!"

Sunif shook his shoulders and wisely informed his younger brother, "Yes, they are great travelers. Sometimes they live in the far, far north. When it is cold, they move their camp far, far to the south."

In a great flurry of feathers and pine needles the Goose Nation circled and then landed in the meadow near the brothers.

"I think I will do something." Mused the older brother, and he loped off to the camp of the geese.

"My relatives," he greeted them, "I would like to

---

92   Fowler, *Anthropology of the Numa* 88-89. Smith, *Ute Tales* 27-28.

travel as you do. I would like to go on a long journey. Give me some feathers from your wings so that I may do this thing."

Each goose plucked a feather and gave it to *Sunif*. He made wings for himself and followed the Goose people as they flapped their wings and rose into the sky. Wolf flapped his wings and followed as they spiraled upward, and then formed into an arrowhead pointed south.

"*Sunif* is a great warrior. Why have we done this thing for him? We are on our way to do battle, but he is much to be feared! He is a great warrior," said the Chief of the Goose People.

Soon Wolf became weary of flapping his wings. His flight wavered and he fluttered, unsteady in his flight. At this the Goose People darted about him, snatching his feathers away until he fell to the ground.

Sunif didn't move. His head hurt and he felt sick and dizzy so he laid there for a long time, not moving. Then he saw a bowl of corn mush on the ground nearby, so he ate it, and when he finished the dizziness and strange feeling only increased. When he put his hand on his head he found that his skull was broken and his hand was covered with his own brains. He then realized that the bowl was his own head and the mush was his own brains, and this made him so sick that he vomited. This was the first time that *Sunif* had tasted food.

"This is something new for me," he mused. "It was good to eat. It was good until I knew it was my own brain. But now I know the pleasure of food."

Now his head was clear, now his body was strong again. He rose to his feet and started at a trot after the Goose Nation. He traveled many days always keeping the sun on his left side. Finally, he found the Goose camp. Coming near, he saw that a great battle had taken place. The geese had killed many people and the bodies were heaped in piles. Then he saw something interesting. He saw a little child in an old woman's arms. *Sunif* had never seen a child before. This was a great curiosity.

"What is this little person? Why is it so small?" he asked the Goose Chief.

"Well, take it home and learn for yourself!" He was angry and tired from the battle.

"How shall I take it, on my feet?"

"No," he said. "For then you cannot walk."

"How shall I carry it, in my arms?"

"No, for then you cannot shoot an arrow."

"Now then, shall I carry it on my back?"

"No, for then it will fall."

Then he said again, "How shall I carry it?"

"Carry it in your belly!"

So he swallowed it and made the long journey home.

After nine moons, the child was born.

"*Aieee! Aieee!*" *Sunif* cried in pain as the child came out of him and gulped its first air.

Since this time this is how children have been born. This is how two-leggeds come into the world, always with pain.

Sunif saw that this child was a girl and so he took her as his wife.

"These birth pains are more than men can endure! From now on only the women will give birth to the children."

WHAT CAN WE LEARN FROM "THE FIRST CHILD BORN"?

I think that this story brings a smile to every woman who has given birth and knows the pain of bringing new life into the world. However, I feel that it also has another purpose. Perhaps it teaches men to regard women with respect. That they can be just as brave in their own way, for what man could undergo the pains of childbirth? This equality of the sexes is another facet of Ute culture that is ahead of its time. The Creator is always spoken of as "He/She." Gender is an animalistic attribute, and the Creator is far beyond such limitations. This theological concept is quite advanced for its time and is a tribute to the cosmology of the Ute.

Another highly advanced concept is the omnipresence of Great Spirit. As was mentioned earlier, Powell and others mistook this to mean worship of animals, or the earth, or the sun. It is much more complex, however, and represents a unitheistic theology. Wolf often takes on the role of Great Spirit. Clifford explained it best:

> Great Spirit, the Creator, is everywhere and in everything. He/She is always present. When Creator wanted to take on physical form, He/She used the form of Wolf. That's why Wolf represents Creator in our stories.[93]

I was puzzled by the key role that Wolf plays in Ute cosmology. However, Clifford explained that the Ute were hunter-gatherers first and foremost. In this lifeway, wolf plays a key role. When wolf is near, it means that game (food) is near. Wolf signals the proximity of elk, deer, antelope, buffalo, etc. Wolf therefore means food

93   Author Interview, Clifford Duncan , 3/10/1998.

and life for the people. Wolf leads the way, showing the best places for hunting. Who hasn't felt shivers go up and down their spine when they hear wolf howl? For the Ute, these shivers, these goose bumps, are an indication of Creator's presence. No wonder Wolf holds such an honored place in Ute cosmology.

The Cannibal 94

There was a very large man. He had a big head, a fat belly, and long feet. He had two wives. His women worked hard gathering seeds. They placed these seeds on a large flat stone on the ground. Then one woman used a small stone to crush the seeds. She then gave these to her sister who placed the crushed seeds on a second flat stone where she also used a small stone to crush them into even smaller bits. They placed this meal in a cooking jar, added a little water, and this made all their meals. They had no game, they had nothing else to eat.

One day the man said to his wives, "Let us go back to where the sun rises. I am tired of eating this grass-seed. I am tired of seeing no tracks and of seeing no game; therefore I wish to go east."

They began their journey the next day, always traveling toward the rising sun. They came to a mountain, working hard to climb to its top, and then traveled down its other side. They were hot and thirsty, and glad to find a spring where they made camp. The next day they rested.

"Stay here. I will go on and hunt," the man told his wives.

The tall man carefully searched the ground for any sign of game. At last he came upon the tracks of a man, a woman, and two children.

"I saw the tracks of four persons," he told his wives when he returned. "I shall go and look for them; perhaps

94   Uintah-Ouray Ute Tribe 81.

we shall see them living somewhere."

His wives followed him to the place where he had seen the tracks. They saw two antelopes.

"Kill them! I am hungry," said one of the women.

"No, they belong to him." And he pointed with his lips to the tracks of the people he was following. They again followed this trail and again camped at a spring.

"I will go after that man and kill him. I want to eat him. I shall bring him back and you also will like to eat him." He followed the man's trail, watching the tracks closely. When he came upon the man, he shot him with his bow. Then he shot the woman and choked the children. He went back to his camp by the spring.

"Let us go there. I have killed them all. We will go to butcher them." His wives skinned and butchered the man and woman, but the cannibal cautioned them, "Skin the boy neatly and carefully. I will do something." They remained at this camp for two days, hanging the meat to dry. The man ate all the meat.

"Stay here, I will travel about to see if I can find anything. I will take the skin of that boy with me." The man left the camp and began to hunt again, climbing a mountain. He looked far below and all around but saw nothing. Then he raised his head a little higher and saw a teepee with two women and a man nearby. The man had stuffed the skin of the boy with grass and now held it up high and moved it around. The second time he did this the man below saw it.

"A boy is up there. Did you see him? I will go up to him." He climbed the mountain and found the boy on the ground. The cannibal hid in the bushes nearby.

"Who are you? Get up. Can you not sit up?" While the man questioned the boy, the cannibal took careful aim from his hiding place and shot him, too. He ran a little way before he fell and died. Now the cannibal ran to another hill. He held the boy in front of a cedar and

moved the boys arm.

"Did you see that boy? He is over there!" A young man who was with the women now dashed up the hill. The cannibal laid the boy down and shot this one as he had shot the other. Then he moved behind another cedar tree and again moved the boy's arm. But the women did not come.

"We will both stay here and wait until the men come," they said.

So the cannibal made a circle to the other side of the teepee. Again he hid behind a tree and moved the boy's arm.

"Who are you? What tribe are you?" called one of the women. The boy disappeared for a moment and then appeared beside another tree. Still the women would not come, so the cannibal circled around and approached the teepee.

"Where is your husband?" he asked.

"He went there after a boy," one woman pointed with her lips. "A young man also went away after that one and has not come back. Maybe that boy was only playing."

While the women looked toward the tree with the boy the cannibal drew his bow and shot them both, one after the other. He picked up the stuffed boy and went back to his teepee.

"I killed four pieces of game." They went to the camp of his victims and the cannibal ate one of the men.

"Gather the bones and get the marrow," he said. Soon they were all fat from eating grease and marrow.

After three sleeps, the cannibal picked up his bow and started off. "I will kill another one for you now. You stay here and I will go hunting." He picked up the boy's skin and started on his way. Again, he climbed another hill and saw an old man, a woman, and a girl below. He hid behind a cedar tree and showed the boy as before.

"I see a boy there. I will go to see what kind of a boy

is there," said the old man as he started up the hill. The cannibal's arrow soon pierced his heart and he dropped to the ground. Then he picked up the boy and showed him again.

"Let us go to see who the boy is. Perhaps someone is living on the other side of the hill now." So the old woman and the girl went to find the boy. The cannibal was hiding behind some cedars and shot them both. He went to their teepee but there was no one there. He had killed them all. He returned to his camp and got his women and they moved to the camp of the victims. After three sleeps the cannibal picked up his bow and the stuffed boy again.

"Stay here," he told his wives. "I will hunt again."

He traveled far but found no one. He grew tired as the sun reached the middle of the sky, so he went to a spring and drank. With his belly full of water he lay down with the boy's skin beside him and was soon asleep.

Two men came to the spring and found the sleeping cannibal.

"Aieee! What is this?"

"He is a bad man! See what he has done to this boy?" They turned and ran as fast as they could but their cries awakened the cannibal. He shot one but the other one escaped.

When the cannibal returned to his camp he told his wives, "I killed one at the spring, let us go there. One of them escaped." His women began to cry.

"Why do you cry?" he asked.

"Because you let him escape. I want him."

"Oh!" he said. "I will get him later."

The man who escaped came to his people's camp. "I saw a bad person. He has a big belly, a big head, and big feet. I saw that he had the skin of a boy. He is bad." They all went to the next camp and told the people there. These also were afraid and went to another place. Thus,

153

they all went away being very afraid. Only in one camp there remained a young man and his mother.

"Let us flee, my son. He is a bad person. He will kill us."

"No, we will stay here. I want to talk to that one. I think he is my friend."

"Son, I am frightened! We must go away before he comes!"

"Now, Mother, get water in a large basket." They lived on a hill made of slate and on this he made a small lake with the water that his mother brought. Ten times she brought him water and he poured it in.

"Mother, now you must take that basket of seeds and cook them."

"I am afraid! I will run away!" she said after she had done as he asked.

"No, my mother, do not fear him. Let him come. He will not hurt you. Go and set fire to that cedar so that he will see the smoke and come to visit us."

When the man saw the smoke he told his wives, "Someone is over there. I saw smoke."

"Good! You will kill him!"

"I will go there now, perhaps there are many people. I will stay there one night, perhaps I will kill ten. If I do not come back after one night you must come after me."

He was hungry so he traveled fast, climbing one hill and then another. At the top, he looked down. The young man was looking for him.

"Look, Mother, there is that man!"

"Oh, my son, I will run away!"

When the cannibal raised the stuffed boy the young man cried out, "Why do you do that? Come here, you."

The cannibal set the skin down and went down to the young man's teepee.

"He is coming now! Let us run!" cried the mother.

"No! Come back, my mother! Let him come. Give him this food."

She was shaking when she came back.

Now the cannibal arrived and the young man went up to him quickly.

"Well, my friend," he said, taking his hand so he could not get his bow. "Sit down there." And the man with the large belly sat down there. "Are you hungry?"

"Yes!"

"What do you wish? Do you want meat or something else?"

"Anything!"

"Very well. Do you like this food? It is already cooked." And the young man gave him a basketful. The cannibal drank all the gruel down.

"Have you finished?"

"No." So the young man gave him another basketful. Again the man drank this off.

"Where do you live? Where is your teepee? Why did you come here?"

"I live far away. I came here with no purpose."

"Stay here one night. We will talk together."

"No, I will go home."

"I have a pretty eagle here on this cliff. Do you wish to see it?" asked the young man.

Then the large-bellied one lay down and looked over the rocky cliff to see the eagle. The young man threw him down into the lake. He swam round and round but could not climb up the steep walls to get out. The young man watched him. Soon he tired and his head went under the water. He came up once again but was too tired. At last he drowned.

The next day the young man stayed at home.

"Where is your rope? What did you do with it? I wish to pull that man out."

"No! He is a bad man!"

"Give me the rope! I will do what is good." And she handed him her yucca rope. He went down to the water and tied the legs and the hands of the man. Then he pulled him out of the water and butchered and skinned him.

"Mother, now you must dry this meat."

"Son, why do you do this?"

"I think that his women will come. We will give them his meat to eat and go outside. We will watch what they do."

He laid two large, fat pieces of the big-bellied man on the stone by the teepee, then went behind a rock and watched. Soon, the two women came. They saw the meat drying on the rack and the cooked meat on the stone, so they sat down and ate.

"Perhaps my husband went to kill the others. He has already killed a fat one." They ate the meat and licked their lips.

"My husband cooks well," said the other wife.

"I am sleepy," said the first wife, yawning.

"I am sleepy too." And they both lay down and went to sleep. Suddenly one jumped up.

"Get up, my sister! My heart is bad, it hits me hard. I think I ate the flesh of my husband!"

"Yes, I also feel bad. I do not know what is the trouble. I think the same as you think."

"Aieee! Aieee!" they both began to wail. The young man was watching and came up to them.

"What is the matter with you? Why do you not eat this meat hanging here? Your husband has gone away hunting."

Behind their hands they said to one another, "Perhaps he killed our husband."

"Yes, I killed your husband. He is a bad man. I will kill you also."

"No, do not kill me!"

"Yes, I will kill you." And he shot them both.

"That one has killed many persons but now he is gone. He is killed. People will not do this anymore. They will be friends and will not eat each other. That one was insane."

WHAT CAN WE LEARN FROM "THE CANNIBAL"?

This legend introduces the extremely controversial subject of cannibalism among the early peoples of the Southwest. In 1999, the topic was most recently brought to light in the Turners' highly controversial book *Man Corn*[95] that caused a firestorm among archaeologists and the public when it was published. Most scientists refused to believe that the Anasazi culture embraced the eating of people. However, when we examine the ethnographic data provided in various Ute legends we find five[96] that have cannibalism as a motif. This is an unusually large number, as no other subject receives the same repetition. Clearly, cannibalism was indelibly etched on the Ute psyche. But why? Was it terrible, but common? Had their ancestors, the Anasazi, been cannibals? Were the Turners correct in their assumptions?

To answer the last question, we must remember that the Anasazi culture was derived from the Toltec-Aztec, as discussed in previous legends, especially "Wolf and Stone Shirt Have a Fight on the Mountain." In this context, we must also remember what we have already learned from Toltec-Aztec burial rites. Defleshing, chopping, cooking, and pulverizing bones to prepare a loved one's body for reincarnation could very easily be interpreted as cannibal activity. How can one tell the difference? This again emphasizes the importance of combining archaeological data with ethnographic data, especially regarding cosmology.

When we study these five legends concerning cannibalism, we find important clues as to the identity of the perpetrators.

---

95   Christy G. Turner, *Man Corn: Cannibalism and Violence in the Prehistoric American Southwest* (Utah UP, 1999).
96   Smith, *Ute Tales* "The Cannibal Bird" 40, "The Man Who Married a Cannibal" 118, *and* "The Cannibals," 120.Uintah-Ouray Ute Tribe "The Cannibal" 81. Fowler "The Cannibal Bird" 269-270.

In "The Cannibal Bird," Owl, a cannibal who carries off a boy, turns into a *big man*. This is similar to the description given in this legend as the cannibal being a "very large man." This coincides with the description of the cannibal tribe given by Coronado's chronicler, Castaneda:

> ...Don Rodrigo Maldonado, who was captain of those who went in search of the ships, did not find them, but he brought back with him an Indian so large and tall that the best man in the army reached only to his chest. It was said that other Indians were even taller on that coast.[97] ...Captain Melchior Diaz... took guides and went toward the north and west in search of the seacoast. After going about 150 leagues, they came to a province of exceedingly tall and strong men – like giants...On account of the great cold, they [giants] carry a firebrand (tison) in the hand when they go from one place to another, with which they warm the other hand and the body as well, and in this way they keep shifting it every now and then. On this account the large river which is in that country was called Rio del Tison (Firebrand River) [The Colorado River].[98]

This location fits with several of the legends which tell of the cannibals who "live to the west." In Smith's "The Cannibals," a small family escapes the cannibals and finds safety in another camp.

"The chief said, 'Yes, many of our men have gone in that direction [west] and never returned...Maybe those cannibals have been killing our men."[99]

---

97 Pedro Reyes Castaneda, *The Journey of Coronado: 1540-1542* 25.

98 Castaneda, 27-28.

99 Castaneda, 120.

Again, in this story of "The Cannibal," he is described as "a big man." This consistency of describing the cannibals as very large men who live in the west fits with Castaneda's reports of the giant Indians who lived near the mouth of the Colorado River, west of the Colorado Plateau. Coincidently, the Turners cite Gifford's (1936) narrative of cannibalism by Yavapai warriors for ethnographic documentation.[100] The Yavapai traditional territory is in southwestern Arizona along the Colorado River.

Early people were highly mobile and therefore is it quite plausible that the Turners' more credible cannibalism incidents can be attributed to roving bands of these cannibals. This is corroborated by this Ute legend's condemnation of cannibalism: "That one has killed many persons, but now he is gone. He is killed. People will not do this anymore. They will be friends and will not eat each other. That one was insane."

Anasazi historian Paul Reed writes, "Much has been made of the apparent lack of burials in Chaco Canyon sites...we have to look for another explanation for the absence of burials..."[101] As discussed in Chapter 15, Toltec-Aztec burial practices may explain this paucity of Anasazi burials. If you de-flesh the body, chop and cook the bones, pulverize them, and then place them in water for a rapid reincarnation, you will not have a burial.

In the next Chapter, we will continue this discussion on cannibalism, as we examine evidence of additional, disturbing factors that may have been overlooked by the Turners and other archaeologists.

---

100   Turner, *Man Corn* 299.
101   Paul F. Reed, editor, *Chaco's Northern Prodigies: Salmon, Aztec, and the Ascendancy of the Middle San Juan Region After AD 1100* (Utah UP, 2008) 57.

Coyote and Beaver [102]

O uwich (Beaver) lived in this water. Right in the center he had a home. A big dome. You go into the water and you swim, dive, to go into the house that was his home. He had children. A lot of children. They would all be playing around the pond.

One day, along the shore came the younger brother of wolf, *Yohowitz* (coyote). He was walking along the edge of the water, the big pond, thinking where his next meal would come from. And as he was walking along he noticed that in the middle of the big pond there was this mound. And he was watching the little beavers swimming around and splashing their tails and making a lot of noise. Laughing.

Coyote watched them for a while thinking of how delicious they would taste. And then from way out there, over on the other side, was the father swimming toward the kids. When Beaver noticed Coyote, he swam toward him. "Hello my friend!" *Ouwich* called out to him. "Come into the water! Come into my home! Let's go sit down."

Coyote answered back, "I don't want to get my fur wet. I don't know how to dive or swim."

"Oh. Maybe I can teach you. Just hold your nose so you don't get water down your nostrils and down your throat and into your body. Just follow me."

Coyote had been thinking about his next meal and how he was going to get it. And he thought to himself, *Now I'm going to get it. This is where it's going to come*

---

102   Legend told by Clifford Duncan, recorded and transcribed by the author 9/11/2003

from. So he held his breath and dove down into the water. The water was cold. Deep into the water he followed the big beaver. He followed him into a dark tunnel that went into the hole. Finally they came into this big dome that had a lighted area. There was a pool there and half of it was built up with mud and dirt, so they came onto this dry area. This was where the beaver lived. They then sat down on the ground. And Coyote was looking around trying to figure out what was going on. He had never been into one of these places. Never been into a beaver's home. The children had followed them and they were swimming around inside the beaver lodge.

Finally he said, "Well, I think that I'm going to go home. I've had enough of this visit."

Beaver said, "Oh, no. You must stay for dinner. I'm going to fix you something to eat."

Coyote felt good because that's what he wanted. His dream was coming true. Over here was a fire and hot charcoal, and near the hot charcoal was a beaver woman, the beaver's wife. *What's cooking? Something – but only for her.*

Coyote looked around. *There's nothing to eat.* But he said, "Okay, I'll eat. I'll stay and eat."

Beaver called his wife and said, "We must prepare a meal for our guest, Coyote is going to stay and eat with us."

"*Heeeey,*" said Beaver. "*Heeeey. Bakhe!* Come here." He called out to one of the kids, one of the children that was swimming around. And one of them swam over. The biggest and fattest one swam over and he had a name that meant "Just Dies." That was his name. And as he came up on top of the deck Beaver picked up a rock and hit him over the head. And down he went. Dead. Beaver then gave him to his wife. "Here. Fix this meal for our guest."

And Coyote just stared. *How could he just do that? One of his own children!* Remember his name was Just Dies. That was his name, Just Dies. He could die anywhere, that was his name. Coyote was in shock because his new friend killed his child for them to eat. At the same time he was confused. *How could a man do that with his own children in his own home?*

Beaver's wife prepared him – put him over the charcoals. Finally, he was ready to eat. It smelled good. Everything was all just right. Coyote came out of his shock for before him was a meal that smelled so good. And Beaver told him, "Okay, you can eat my friend. You're my friend."

Coyote didn't know what to do. Beaver said, "Don't be afraid. Eat it, like this." And he grabbed a piece of meat and started chewing on it.

"But you must do it like this. When you eat that meat, don't throw away the bones. You must pile them neatly over here. You must clean that meat off and put that neatly cleaned bone over here. Pile them all together."

So Coyote ate. It was really good. "Yes, it tastes good." So he piled all of the bones to one side, as he was told. When they were through eating they sat around and relaxed and started talking again. They took a pipe and smoked and told stories. Coyote didn't feel good because he still couldn't understand how the whole thing worked. But he was happy because he had his meal. And just when he was about to leave Beaver said, "Wait. Before you go, let's do this." And he picked up all the bones that were neatly piled. Beaver then threw them into the water. And as the bones touched the water all together they turned back into the boy again and Just Dies swam back to the rest of the kids. Now, Coyote burst with a new idea.

Well, Coyote thought. *Nobody is going to beat me. Being such a powerful man, I can do the same trick that he did. If he can do it, I can do it too. I have learned something today.*

165

Without further hesitation he invited the beaver to his house. "You must come to my house." And he told him where he lived. "I live way out there – there's a big lake. That's where I live. You have to dive into the water and swim to come into my house." He was thinking of a place where he had been several days before, and he gave Beaver directions as which way to get there. In reality, he didn't have that house or live in the water. So quickly he went dashing down to the lake and built his home. Gathered all his kids in there.

Finally, the day arrived that Beaver paid him a visit. He came to this pond, this big lake, and out in the middle there was a big mound made out of sticks and mud. Over to the left Coyote was patiently waiting, sitting by the shore. Then he dove into the water and came swimming back. Then he told Beaver, "You must dive into the water and come into my house. You have to dive into the water and come up through the tunnel and up into my home."

It was exactly like Beaver's house inside. He had copied the man down to the last detail, even his kids were swimming around inside. His wife was cooking a meal for herself. And after a while as he and Beaver were talking about certain things he said, "You must get ready. We are going to eat after a while." And he called out to one of his big kids – he had the same name, Just Dies, just like the beaver child with that same name. Then Coyote did the same thing that Beaver had done. He called out, saying "Heeey, Elich, *Bakhe*. Come Here." And one of the coyote kids swam over with his big, bushy tail swinging behind him. Then Coyote hit "Just Dies" over the head. Killed him. He told his wife to prepare their meal. The wife fixed it and gave it to the two as they were sitting on the ground. He said to Beaver, "You must pile the bones over here on the ground." He thought to himself, *No one is going to beat me. No one is going to outdo Coyote.*

They got through eating and then the time arrived

when Beaver wanted to go home. Coyote said, "Wait. Let's put these back in the water." And he threw the bones into the water. Big splash! But nothing happened. The bones sank down to the bottom. Coyote had murdered one of his children.

The moral of the story is this: Don't ever do what other people do because it may not work for you. So when you see people do certain things that aren't right, or look different, don't go ahead and do that, because what may work for them may not work for you. What others may do may not be possible for you to do.

WHAT CAN WE LEARN FROM "COYOTE AND BEAVER"?

"Coyote and Beaver" is perhaps one of the most important legends in this collection. I feel that it holds the key to the collapse of the Anasazi culture and the origins of the Ute People.

It is my hypothesis – based on extensive ethnographic, archaeological and historical data – that the Chaco culture was destroyed by religious warfare.

Historian Steven LeBlanc speaks to this very issue:

An interesting alternative [in explaining the collapse of Anasazi culture] ...is a "peaceful until near the end" model. This model theorizes that the Chaco system was participatory without coercion. The populace willingly provided labor and resources for maintaining the centers, roads, and other labor-intensive facilities....Then, sometime in the early 1100s, the system began to break down...This model has a good deal to recommend it, but it would require evidence for violence to appear only late in the interval...[103]

Whatever the cause for the cultural changes that took place around A.D. 1150 – the collapse of the Chaco Interaction Sphere, the end of the Classic Mimbres, and the abrupt change in the long-standing Hohokam cultural tradition – they seem to be associated with a return to a visible level of warfare.[104]

For almost 300 years, prior to A.D. 1150, the Anasazi experienced something that has been labeled "Pax Chaco"–an extended period of peace. Archaeologist Stephen Lekson comments on this unusual period in

---

103   Steven A. LeBlanc, *Prehistoric Warfare in the American Southwest* (Utah UP,1999) 184.
104   LeBlanc, 195.

Anasazi history.

Steven LeBlanc chronicled the escalating levels of feuding and raiding in the eighth and ninth centuries. With the rise of Chaco, that violence suddenly ended. A remarkable era of peace – which someone illiterate in Latin dubbed the Pax Chaco – blessed the countryside from 900 to 1250.[105]
...Outliers – colony or copy Great Houses – popped up, up to 250 kilometers [approx. 155 miles] away [from Chaco]. Local leaders almost everywhere on the [Colorado] Plateau joined with or deferred to Chaco. And it worked. The weather cooperated; rain fell. From 900 to 1200, Chaco kept the peace, promoted the General welfare, enhanced its own glory, and got things done.[106]

Again, we can gain some insight into this remarkable, peaceful transition when we consider an integrated history of North and South America. When Teotihuacan (an early Toltec center)[107] fell in 650 A.D., as many as 60,000 people dispersed, many going north.[108] Most Anasazi archaeologists have acknowledged the Toltec link to Chaco, but Lekson said it best: "Almost every consideration of this question moves from south to north, sometimes very specifically from Tula [Toltec capital] to Chaco. Mesoamerica was the cause, and Chaco the effect."[109]
The synchronicity of the fall of Teotihuacan and the founding of Chaco corroborates Lekson's statement. I would propose that this influx at Chaco was the first wave

105   Lekson, A *History of Ancient Southwest* 128-129.
106   Lekson, 235.
107   Brien Foerster, Mysterious Toltec Civilization of Mexico. Retreived from (http://hiddenincatours.com)
108   Lekson, A *History*, 79-80.
109   Lekson, 139.

of Toltec religious refugees and that they established themselves at Chaco while maintaining their connections to relatives in Mexico.

I propose that a second wave of refugees arrived in Chaco in the early 900s, and that this religious sect was responsible for "Pax Chaco." This seems quite logical when we examine the life of the legendary Topiltzin Quetzalcoatl. When he abdicated his throne in Tollan, he then began his migrations about the year 883 AD.[110] Topiltzin Quetzalcoatl's empire was based at Teotihuacan, which the Mayans called "Puh" or Place of Reeds (Tulan/Tollan).[111] The very name "Toltec" means a person from Tollan.[112] If we consider this scenario then the peaceful assimilation of the inhabitants in the áreas surrounding Chaco is easily explained.

Unfortunately, something radically shifted in the early 1200s, and a new religion surfaced at Chaco. Anasazi archaeologist Paul F. Reed is one of the first to broach this subject, writing that "...we could infer that the Katsina cult, which radically changed Western Pueblo social organization in the 1300s C.E. ... developed initially at Chaco Canyon...[113]"

University of Arizona historian, Susan E. James further explores the origins of the kachina cult in the "Journal of the Southwest." She writes that "The kachina cult seems to have been imported from Mexico in roughly a 200-year period from 1250-1470 C.E., a time of extreme drought on the Colorado Plateau."[114] James also connects

---

110   H.B. Nicholson, *Topiltzin Quetzalcoatl: The Once and Future Lord of the Toltecs* (Colorado UP, 2001) 273.
111   Linda Schele & Peter Mathews, *The Code of Kings: The Language of Seven Sacred Maya Temples and Tombs* (Touchstone by Simon & Schuster, 1998) 200.
112   Schele, *The Code of Kings* 200.
113   Paul F. Reed, *Puebloan Society of Chaco Canyon* (Greenwood Press, 2001) 141.
114   Susan E. James, "Some Aspects of the Aztec Religion in the

the Hopi, descendants of the Anasazi, Powamu Ceremony with the very similar Aztec ceremony for rain.

> The purpose of the rituals was to bring rain and encourage fertility during the spring planting season. To this end, incense, rubber, food, and pulque were offered to the gods, but more particular to these rites were the offerings of the blood of children, both from small, localized perforations – such as the tongue, ear, or shin – and from actual child sacrifice.[115]

Empirical evidence of this ceremony is best exemplified by the events at the Tower Kiva in Salmon Ruins in 1263. Archaeologist John Kantner cites a study by Irwin-Williams and Shelley.

> At Salmon, an old Chaco-era great house reoccupied in the thirteenth century, 45-55 individuals, mostly children [33], were burned in the central tower kiva around AD 1263 (Irwin-Williams and Shelley 1980).[116]

Steven LeBlanc also made note of this great tragedy.

> At Salmon ruin, one of the more tragic events of this period apparently occurred: Thirty-three children perished in a tower kiva, sometime after A.D. 1263 and before the end of the century. The best reconstruction of this catastrophe is that the children were on the roof of a tower kiva, which then burned, along with much of the site.[117]

Hopi Kachina Cult," *Journal of the Southwest* 897.
115   Susan E. James, "Mimetic Rituals of Child Sacrifice in the Hopi Kachina Cult," *Journal of the Southwest*.
116   John Kantner, *Ancient Puebloan Southwest* (Cambridge UP, 2004) 169-171.
117   LeBlanc, *Prehistoric Warfare* 233.

This disproportionate ratio of children to adults clearly indicates a ritual, and there are at least fifteen other Anasazi archaeological sites with a similar child victim scenario. Is it merely a coincidence that so many children are found dead upon the arrival of the kachina religion?

> Most significant, perhaps, was the finding of a carved, green sandstone lizard [salamander] effigy near the floor of the Tower Kiva. Research into Puebloan ethnography suggested that the effigy represented Lizard Woman...[118]

We can safely assume that the effigy of Lizard Woman is actually a salamander based on the four toes represented on the carving. A lizard has five. Salamander is a traditional symbol of birth and regeneration in the Pueblo world. The Colorado Plateau is the natural habitat for the Tiger Salamander which is able to regenerate a lost limb, emerge unburned from fires, and seemingly come back to life after hibernating through the winter. Salamanders also cannibalize their young. Is it simply a coincidence that this fetish was placed so prominently with the children's remains in Tower Kiva?

It seems to me that this tragedy at Salmon Ruins clearly echoes Clifford's legend of beaver eating his children in the belief that they will come back to life. Is it any wonder, then, that the Chaco world blew apart. Why would we suddenly see evidence of child sacrifice at Chaco and the coincident abandonment of Chaco Canyon? Religious warfare would seem a quite logical explanation. If a new religion arrived at the same time as a major drought, and promised that sacrificing children

---

118   Reed, *Puebloan Society of Chaco Canyon* 66.

would bring rain, then there was undoubtedly a faction that was won over. It is equally probable that another large faction militantly resisted such a drastic solution to drought. Religious warfare is the logical outcome of such a situation.

I propose that when Chaco was abandoned in the early 1200s the two religious factions moved north to Salmon (kachina) and northeast to Aztec (Toltec). Reed contrasts the two settlements in his *Puebloan Society of Chaco Canyon.*

> At Aztec, construction efforts were less intense, but the drive to maintain Chacoan standards is seen in the construction of Aztec East through the AD 1100s and into the 1200s, an effort not duplicated at Salmon.[119]

Stuart corroborates this observation, giving further proof of the intentional separation of Salmon culture from Chaco culture.

> In contrast to Chaco Canyon, where pottery was imported, artisans made most of the pottery at Salmon Ruin locally. This pottery even included an inexact local copy of the late Gallup Black-on-white style so favored in the central basin at this time. Why wasn't true Chacoan pottery in abundance at Salmon Ruin?[120]

It would seem that the people of Salmon were making a deliberate break with Chaco architecture and the physical culture, as well as Chaco itself, while Aztec took the opposite track. Why? I propose that this is further evidence of the religious warfare. Reed illustrates this difference further in his book *Chaco's Northern*

119   Reed, *Puebloan Society of Chaco Canyon* 136.
120   Stuart, *Anasazi America* 84

Prodigies.

If Steve Lekson (1999) ...are correct, Aztec was founded by Chacoan groups intent on re-creating the complex of great houses and ritual structures that formed "downtown" Chaco Canyon.[121]

Lekson explains what happens next.

But a fifty-year drought from 1130-1180 showed that at least two generations of Aztec leaders failed in their jobs. Dissent and unrest stirred the countryside ... Archaeology reveals about two-score mass executions of families or small settlements, with great brutality and even desecratory cannibalism. (Turners 1999) I use the word unspeakable literally and ironically. These were acts of appalling violence, differing from twentieth-century cruelties only in scale. One cannot imagine the horror of extended families cut to ribbons and their bodies, in pieces, tossed into kivas (Turner and Turner 1999; White 1992). I believe that these executions were public and meant to intimidate villagers from the surrounding countryside.[122]

And so we have it. Religious warfare – the Kachina cult against the Chacoan Toltecs. The Toltec religion, as established by the near-mythical Topilzin Quetzalcoatl, expressly forbid human sacrifice, a diametrical opposition to the kachina religion. Harvard historian H. B. Nicholson writes of Topiltzin Quetzalcoatl.

Under his benevolent rule no human sacrifice was permitted, only that of quail, butterflies, snakes, and large grasshoppers. Threatened by the gods

121   Reed, *Chaco's Northern Prodigies* 24.
122   Lekson, *A History* 160 (fn p308).

Huitzilopochtli and Tezcatlipoca (or their human partisans), who demanded human victims, Topiltzin, refusing to change his policy, departed Tollan, accompanied by many of his people...[123]

After these Toltec religious refugees abandoned Chaco they re-established themselves at Aztec. However, the religious wars escalated, and after devastating attacks on Aztec, they fled northwest to Mesa Verde. Lekson explains this turbulent period in Anasazi history.

The new capital [Aztec] was unable to keep the peace or to bring the rain as Chaco had done. A major drought hit from 1135 to 1180 ...But about 1250 rainfall became erratic and unpredictable. At 1275 an even worse drought began; it would last for a quarter century...Violence spun out of control. Farmsteads – previously scattered freely among their fields – clustered into large, walled towns or huddled together in alcoves high on the cliffs of Mesa Verde.[124]

And Lekson gives us another insight into this religious war that again points to the kachina religion.

Violence did not end with the migrations [late 1100s] out of the northern San Juan [Chaco]... Violence flared. Wars broke out, with villages sacking other villages...New images of kachinas and other supernaturals bloomed on pottery and rock art like flowers after rain...The macaw, whose feathers had once distinguished Pueblo nobles, became a close affiliate of kachinas.[125]

---

123   Nicholson *Topiltzin Queztalcoatl* 10.
124   Lekson, *A History* 239.
125   Lekson, *A History* 242.

Stuart augments this theory of religious warfare writing that these were religious pilgrims: "... these great houses [Mesa Verde] and others farther north were founded by groups of male colonists, the religious elites, who migrated out of Chaco Canyon in the 1120s."[126]

Fortunately, after generations of these religious wars, something shifted in the late 1200s. After 1280, no more wood is cut at Mesa Verde and the defensive cliff dwellings are abandoned.[127] Why? And it wasn't only the buildings that were abandoned – it was also the culture.

Artifacts formerly essential to life in the northern San Juan – ceramic mugs, a distinctive form made almost exclusively in the Mesa Verde area – were never made again. Mugs were not simply for drinking; if they were merely useful forms, everyone would have made them, but only Mesa Verde did. Mugs meant something that people did not want to remember or continue in their new lives. "Keyhole kivas," once requisite architecture at every Mesa Verde home, were likewise made no more.[128]

Why would a civilization change so dramatically? Where did the people go? Language is one of the clues we can use to solve this mystery. If we follow the language we find three distinct areas among modern Uto-Aztecan speakers. They spread along the Rio Grande into western Arizona and into the mountains of Utah and Colorado.

The Kiowa-Tanoan branch of Uto-Aztecan Family disbursed among the following Pueblos:
1. Tiwa (Taos, Picuris, Isleta, Sandia)
2. Tewa (San Juan, Santa Clara, San Ildefonso, Tesuque,

---

126   Stuart, *Anasazi America* 129.
127   Beth and Bill Sagstetter, *The Cliff Dwellings Speak* (Benchmark Publishing of Colorado, 2010) 63.
128   Lekson, *A History* 164.

Nambe, Hano)
3. Towa (Jemez)
4. Kiowa[129]

Among the remaining Uto-Aztecan family members, the Hopi dispersed to their mesa tops in Arizona, and the Ute remained in the Chaco culture area, spreading into the mountains of Utah, Colorado, and northern New Mexico.

Just as we see with modern-day response to religious wars, there was no single response to the upheaval. The collapsing Anasazi culture followed this pattern.

Kiowa-Tanoan speakers fled the area and re-established themselves along the northern Rio Grande to become the modern day Pueblos of that area. Kantner explains the dispersion of these Tanoan groups as follows:

Some scholars contend that "basal" Tanoan was spoken across much of the northern Colorado Plateau, including Mesa Verde and northern Rio Grande areas... Towa oral histories trace their roots to the [San Juan River] area, and Mackey's (1977) skeletal analyses provide some support. Cheryl Ferguson (1980) also found similarities between skeletal remains from the Towa village of Pecos and those from the thirteenth-century occupation of Aztec. Archaeological evidence suggests that these northern residents migrated into the Jemez [New Mexico] region in AD 1300s, where they probably joined local Tanoan speakers...By the time of European Contact, Tewa-speaking people were living in a dozen towns north of the modern city of Santa Fe, as well as in a handful of communities in the Galisteo Basin. Oral histories recount the journey of Tewa people from the northwest – often Mesa Verde is

---

129   Carl Waldman, *Atlas of the North American Indian* (Facts On File Inc., 1985) 68.

indicated – down the Chama and Rio Grande valleys... Archaeological evidence is consistent with these scenarios, for Mesa Verde-style pottery, masonry, and kiva styles are found among thirteenth-century towns of the northern Rio Grande...Historical linguistics suggests that the Tewa language diverged from basal Tanoan around AD 1050-1350...[130]

The Hopi, on the other hand, isolated themselves on three mesas in northeastern Arizona. Archaeology of the area suggests that their villages were established here by the 1300s.[131] Finally, we come to the Ute People.

For many years, archaeologists have placed the blame for warfare and the abandonment of Chaco on the Ute – regardless of their kinship to the Hopi and Puebloan people. They have been cast as outsiders, appearing from somewhere out of the north and wreaking their havoc. Now, however, we are finally coming to a more enlightened understanding of Ute prehistory. In the July, 2003 issue of Smithsonian, author David Roberts quotes William Lipe (an archaeologist at Washington State University).

There's simply no evidence [of nomadic tribes] in the 13th century. This is one of the most thoroughly investigated regions in the world. If there were enough nomads to drive out tens of thousands of people, surely the invaders would have left plenty of archaeological evidence. [132]

Of course there's no evidence of raiding nomadic tribes. The transformation of Anasazi culture was the

---

130   Kantner, *Ancient Puebloan Southwest* 264-265.
131   LeBlanc, *Prehistoric Warfare* 329.
132   John Roberts, "Riddles of the Anasazi," *Smithsonian Magazine*, July 2003.

result of a bitter and violent religious war. Outsiders did not attack and drive them out of their lands. These ancient people chose to segregate and reorganize themselves according to religious beliefs. Human history is riddled with this type of cultural upheaval. Most of the wars throughout the ages are caused by the clash of religious ideals.

Before the Ute People reverted to hunter-gatherers (as they were at Spanish contact), they were the Anasazi. Who among the Uto-Aztecan speaking people of Chaco culture area and Mesa Verde retains a presence in their ancestral area? The Ute People. Who retains long-standing, pre-contact ownership of part of the Mesa Verde region? The Ute People. Who retains the name "The Ancient Ones?" It is the Wiinuuchi (also spelled Weenuche, Weeminuche Band), the Ute Mountain Ute. Their name literally means "The Old People" or "The Old Utes."[133]

Many times I questioned Clifford, "Why are the Ute and the Hopi such bitter enemies? Weren't you one Nation long ago? What happened at Chaco? Why won't you talk about it?" His only response was cryptic. "Bad things happened there. We don't talk about it."

---

133   Ute Dictionary 207.

Coyote's Blind Eyes [134]

O ne day while he was out walking, Coyote came
to a lake where he saw many ducks and geese
swimming around. He crept close to the shore of
the lake and watched them.

They look good to eat, he thought. *I wonder how I
can catch them?* He sat and thought for a long time, and
then decided that he would try walking on the bottom
of the lake. He walked and walked and then he saw the
birds' feet. He reached up and grabbed one and took it to
the shore. He was so hungry that he decided to get more
birds. He kept walking under water, grabbing a winged-
one's feet, and took them back to his pile until he had four
big ones. He carried all of these to his home. He met an
Indian friend when he got there.

"What do you call them?" He asked.

"*Cheeguch*, ducks," said his friend, "and the geese
are *Eevennook*."

"What are they good for?"

"They are good to eat," replied the Indian. "We use
the small feathers for pillows to rest our heads and the
long ones to feather our arrows."

Coyote's stomach hurt, so he cooked the birds and
ate them until his belly was full. Then he made arrows
with the long feathers.

Next, the Indian showed Coyote how to hunt with
a bow and arrow. They went hunting for fish. The Indian

---

134   Unitah-Ouray Ute Tribe 98-101. Smith, *Ute Tales* 5.

shot one.

I *can do that*, thought Coyote. So he left his friend and went hunting alone. He came to a creek and saw many fish swimming. Coyote stood on the bank and a big fish swam just below him. He lifted his bow, notched an arrow, and sent it flying into the fish. *Splash!* The fish jumped into the air, turned on its belly, broke Coyote's arrow, and swam off.

"*Aieee!*" yelped Coyote, and ran back to his camp.

"That big fish broke my arrow! He jumped in the air!" he cried to his Indian friend.

"You must go again. Kill the fish, he is good to eat. You can also dry him and keep his flesh for later."

Coyote wandered away from camp, sniffing the air. Every few steps he turned back, to see if anyone was watching him. He came to some tall pines and he heard laughter and talking. There was a camp of large, black Bear people.

"*Aiyeee!*" yelped Coyote, and ran back to his camp.

"My friend, I need some arrows!" He grabbed his bow and the arrows and ran back to the Bear camp. He kept in the shadows and walked close to their camp with soft moccasins. He could hear them talking.

"Hold on," Bear's wife said. "Coyote may come and see what you are doing."

"Oh, no! Coyote is a coward. He is afraid of everything. If he saw me a long ways off then he would run," laughed Bear.

Coyote notched an arrow in his bow and let it fly. One, two, three, four times.

"*Waughhh!*" Growled Bear. "How did Coyote learn to shoot and hurt me?" Bear ran with Coyote's arrows in his rump. "I'll kill him some time," he said.

"*Yip, yip, yip, yip!*" Coyote laughed and laughed as he chased him.

One moon later, Coyote went wandering around,

sniffing the ground just to see what he could find. He heard someone singing and talking so he crept on soft moccasins into the willows and watched.

"Fee, beee," the *Noonapakutch*, (little chickadees) sang as they pulled their eyes out and threw them up into the willow branches. Berries and fruits rained down and the birds happily pecked along the ground until their bellies were full.

"*Towaoc! Towaoc!* Thank you! Thank you!" sang the *Noonopakutch*. And their eyes fell down and back into their heads again.

"He*yyyy*. What are you doing with your eyes?" asked Coyote.

"Oh, we're just having some fun."

"Let me try it!" begged Coyote.

"No," the little ones answered. "You will lose your eyes. You can't do it."

"My stomach hurts," begged Coyote.

"We will show you. But you may only do it four times. Do not do it more than four."

"*Fee, beee*," sang Coyote as he threw his eyes up into the pines.

Down came the berries and Coyote filled his belly one, two, three, four times.

"*Towaoc! Towaoc!*" sang Coyote. But his eyes hung up in the pine trees. His blind eyes stayed there, they didn't come back. *I am crazy! I cannot see!* he thought. He heard the water rushing in the stream and followed the sound. He sat down among the willows. After a while coyote heard two little girls coming along.

"Halloo! Where do you come from? What tribe do you belong to?" Coyote called to them, for they didn't see him.

"Oh, we are Ute. What tribe are you?"

"Just the same as you – Ute. I'll go along with you."

"All right."

So Coyote covered his eyes and walked along with the girls. Soon they came upon a buffalo.

"Kill it!" cried the girls.

"Yes, but I left my arrows at home."

"Never mind. We'll make one for you." And they made one out of bone. "You'd better kill one!"

Coyote circled around, sniffing the air, until he got downwind from the buffalo. He carefully crawled among the grasses as the scent got stronger. When he knew he was close enough he notched his arrow and let it fly. He hit it and killed it but he did not know he had. He thought he had missed it. He heard the girls come and stand beside him.

"Why don't you skin it?"

"Well, I was waiting for you," he replied and then followed them up to the dead buffalo.

"Why don't you begin?" they asked.

"I haven't any knife." So one of the girls handed hers to him, but he stretched his hands out before him trying to find it.

"What's the matter? Haven't you any eyes?"

Coyote followed her voice and grabbed the knife. He tried to skin the buffalo but shredded it instead as he slashed blindly with the knife.

"What's the matter? You've cut the skin to pieces."

"Oh! I tried to skin it quickly. We'll throw it away and kill some more buffalo."

The girls started a fire and cooked the meat. "Come eat!" they called to him.

Coyote just walked past them, far below their fire.

"Where are you going?"

"Oh, I was just doing that for fun." Coyote sniffed the smoke and followed it. He came as close to the fire as he dared but sat down right in the middle of the meat.

"Why do you sit down in the meat?"

They all filled their bellies with the buffalo, then

the girls built a wickiup and Coyote went in and lay down. Soon he was fast asleep while the girls cleaned up the camp and packed the meat.

What's the reason he can't see? Maybe he has no eyes! they thought as they worked. They looked at each other, shook their heads, and crept into the wickiup. Slowly they lifted his blanket and saw that his eyes were gone. "*Hmmmm.* Coyote has been tricking us," they whispered, and then ran away into the pines. They came to a dead Standing One laying on the ground and rotting. It was full of red ants. They snatched one of its branches up and carried it back to the wickiup. They put it under Coyote's head, and ran off again. Soon Coyote's head was crawling with angry red ants. They crept into his eye sockets and bit him.

"*Aiyeee! Aiyee!*" Coyote awoke with a yelp. "Come here! The ants are biting me all over." Only silence. The girls weren't there. Coyote jumped out of his bed and sniffed the ground until he found the girls' trail. He loped after them with his nose to the ground. They were on a high hill and they saw him coming.

"What's the matter?" they called to him.

"All right," Coyote howled. "I'll catch you!"

"All right," the girls replied and began to run. One of the girls carried a purse on her belt and it had jingles that tinkled as she ran. Coyote followed the sound and came closer and closer. The girls ran to a high cliff and threw the jingle purse over the edge, then ran and hid behind a Standing One. Coyote followed the sound of the jingle purse over the rocky ledge and landed on the boulders below. He broke his leg. The girls carefully walked to the edge and looked over. There was Coyote, far below, eating the marrow of his broken leg.

"Coyote," sang the girls. "What are you doing? Eating your own leg-grease? Shame!"

"No! I killed a mountain sheep and I am eating his bones. Better come down." 185

"No," they called. "You are eating your own leg grease. Shame!"

WHAT CAN WE LEARN FROM "COYOTE'S BLIND EYES"?

As with most of these Ute legends, "Coyote's Blind Eyes" speaks on several different levels. And, just as with most of the Ute cautionary tales, it first emphasizes the importance of carefully listening to instructions. Coyote was emphatically told not to perform the magic more than four times. When he ignored this caution he paid with the loss of his eyes.

The second teaching found in this legend is more grim. In our society, it would be shocking to speak openly of cannibalism to children. However, as shown in previous chapters, this was a serious matter to the Ute, and so the condemnation of such practice is again echoed here. Coyote is again ridiculed for eating his own flesh.

Finally, when we look at this legend in a historical context we can find a vital clue to a turning point in American history, De Anza's Comanche campaign of 1779. This legend provides key information in retracing Anza's route on this campaign.

Two previously published works, *Anza's 1779 Comanche Campaign* by Ron Kessler (2nd Edition, 2001) and *Anza and Cuerno Verde: Decisive Battle* by Wilfred O. Martinez (2001), provide detailed information on this battle and Anza's war trail from Santa Fe to Salida and from Colorado Springs back to Santa Fe. However, the exact route of Anza's expedition from the time that he crossed the Arkansas River at Salida until he engaged the Comanches in combat near the confluence of Fountain and Monument Creeks in Colorado Springs has been more difficult to map.

After carefully examining Anza's journals and other documentation, I propose that the missing section of this route ran from South Park through Florissant and down

Ute Pass. Anza's reference to "Los Ojos Ciegos" (The Blind Eyes) as a landmark is one of the keys to unlocking the riddle. This missing Florissant segment also corroborates both Martinez and Kessler's conclusion that the decisive battle was at America the Beautiful Park in Colorado Springs. Anza's success in this campaign was due in large part because he enlisted two-hundred Ute warriors to guide his army. They alone knew of a back way, a surprise route, which led the Spanish, unseen, through the mountains and down Ute Pass.

His Ute guides were more than willing accomplices. They were out for revenge and retribution after Comanches attacked a peaceful Ute village in South Park. Anza made a record of this attack in his journal entry of July 18, 1779.

> ... a large number of Comanches attacked a larger number of Jutas at this place [near Saguache] where they had located with their families, and although the former succeeded in taking all their horses under the cover of darkness, the latter came off with the advantage, having killed 12 of the thieves, one of them a chief, their bodies bearing better witness to the victory than did the account rendered by the victors.[135]

We can safely assume that the Ute warriors accompanying him were from the Tabeguache-Uncompaghre Band. The incident cited above took place near Saguache, in the heart of Tabeguache-Uncompaghre territory. Anza also tells us that, "The Juta [Ute] tribe that is accompanying us lives in the summertime near that river's [Rio Grande] source..." This also verifies that the warriors were Tabegauche-Uncompaghre because Dominguez and Escalante documented the headwaters of

---

135   Ronald E.Kessler, *Anza's 1779 Comanche Campaign* (Adobe Village Press, 2001).

the Rio Grande as being the territory of the Tabeguache-Uncompaghre in their journals of 1776.[136]

As noted in Chapter 12, the Tabeguache Band takes its name from Pikes Peak, *Tava* in their language. Remember that *Tava* translates as "Sun" and *Tabeguache* translates as the "People of Sun Mountain." This is a critical point as Ute Pass lies along the northern base of Pikes Peak. The 1778 Spanish map of the Pikes Peak area shows Comanche villages just to the east of the Peak.[137] It does not show Ute Pass. However, the first map printed (1795) subsequent to Anza's 1779 campaign shows Ute Pass, labeled as *Puerto del Almagre* (Doorway to the Red Earth Mountains). It also reflects Comanche presence on the plains east, north and south of Pikes Peak.[138]

Anza's use of an (1) an unknown route, (2) Tabeguache guides, and (3) the words "toward a predetermined ultimate route" indicate that his objective was Ute Pass. This reasoning is bolstered by the unique landmarks that he noted in his journal on August 30th.

> ...comenzamos a atravezar la sierra del almagre...fin aun dentro de la misma en un rio que nace que llame Santa Rosa...(we commenced slowly across the Red Earth Mountains...ending among the same on a river that is born there that we called Santa Rosa [Fountain Creek].[139]

This explicit reference to the Red Earth Mountains (Pikes Peak massif) and to the headwaters of Fountain Creek firmly places Anza in Ute Pass on August 30th.

With this information, his journal entry for the previous day, Sunday, August 29, clearly places him in the

---

136   Smith, *Ethnography of the Northern Ute* 5
137   Kaelin, *American Indians of the Pikes Peak Region* 77.
138   Kaelin, *American Indians of the Pikes Peak Region* 76.
139   Kessler, *Anza's 1779 Comanche Campaign* 24.

Florissant Valley: "...bien entrda la noche, al pie de una lomeria, que se uamaron los ojos ciegos. (well into the night, [we made camp] at the foot of a high hill that is called The Blind Eyes.)"[140] This has to be Twin Rocks, the only prominent landmark along the Ute Trail within the region of Anza's march. These twin boulders are clearly Coyote's eyes, hanging in the pine trees where he threw them. The Blind Eyes.

Florissant Valley is a large, grassy meadow that was a lake bed 35 million years ago. Stately Ponderosa pines shroud the backside of Pikes Peak and crowd along the curving edges of the valley. Silica-rich bunch grass and blue grama grass abound, watered by Twin Creek – the only stream, whiskered with willows, that drains the Peak's west slope and meanders toward the Platte River. A centuries-old Ute lodge-pole trail runs from Colorado Springs through Ute Pass, over Hayden's Divide, crosses the valley, and continues into South Park. Early pioneers adapted their travel to this ready-made road and named a landmark boulder escarpment above the valley Twin Rocks. This unique landmark was critical to all travelers, Indians and non-Indians, navigating Pikes Peak backcountry. It safely led the way into the breach in the mountains known as Ute Pass.

Anza's was the first Spanish army to avail itself of this backdoor attack on the Comanche. After coming north from Santa Fe he marched his army at night, safely crossing the San Louis Valley and South Park. After spending the night in the Florissant valley he quartered his massive army at Cascade on Monday, August 30, the night before his decisive battle at America the Beautiful Park.

At first glance, Cascade seems an impossible place to pasture 2,400 head of horses much less camps for 800 men (including 200 Ute scouts and four Ute Chiefs).

140   Kessler, *Anza's 1779 Comanche Campaign* 12, 24.

However, there is an open area above Marigreen Pines that fits all of the requirements for the Spanish army and the description given by Anza:

1. It is large enough for Anza's camp and its horse herd.
2. It provides an excellent vantage point of Comanche territory. Anza writes, "that these heights overlook those customarily inhabited by the enemy [Comanche]"
3. It provides the perfect timing for the Spanish army to dash down to America the Beautiful Park in Colorado Springs. Timing is the only measure we can use for this segment as Anza doesn't give the distance, only the time it took his soldiers to reach the enemy. (As noted earlier, Martinez gives excellent data for locating this battle at American the Beautiful Park and it is now the acknowledged location of the battle.)

Anza's Ute scouts were probably near Manitou Springs, perhaps on Red Mountain or Iron Mountain, when they first spotted the Comanche. He had sent out three separate parties of Ute scouts the day before the attack. He writes that, "at half past ten [Aug 30th] one of those spies told us that to the east of where we were camped" his scouts saw the dust of the Comanche army. Anza mounted up his army, leaving a rear guard of 200 with the horse herd at Cascade. The main army engaged the Comanches about 12:00 p.m. at America the Beautiful Park.

Anza dealt a crushing blow to the Comanche in this first engagement, killing 18 "of the strongest" and wounding many more. He describes some of the action as follows:

...it was necessary to kill more than thirty women and children ...the number of the enemies we fought cannot be arrived at with any certitude, because since the men dress the same as the women with whom they were fleeing, and the horses they were trying to get away with raised so much dust it was impossible to count them. [141]

Anza then took 34 women and children prisoner and captured 500 head of horses. He continued a running battle with the remaining Comanches until a final engagement on August 3rd, when his men killed the Comanche Chief Querno Verde, his son, their Medicine Man, and ten other warriors – breaking the Comanche resistance.

Historically, this 1779 battle against the Comanche was one of the major turning points in the history of the United States. Originally part of the Yamparica Band of Ute, the Comanche split away from the Ute Nation in the early 1700s[142] and went on to become the scourge of the Spanish in North America, very nearly forcing them back into Mexico. The Comanche had a zero tolerance policy toward intruders, and controlled the entire front range of Colorado as well as the Arkansas River and most of northern New Mexico.

Anza could not have won this victory in 1779 without his Ute scouts. They knew the territory like the back of their hand. Other Spanish armies had marched up through Raton or La Veta Pass where the Comanches could spot them days in advance and simply melt into the landscape. The surprise attack through Ute Pass was made possible by the Ute scouts. As noted earlier in this section, Ute Pass was never noted on a Spanish map prior to this battle.

If Anza's army had failed in 1779, the Comanche very likely would have prevented the opening of the Santa

---

141   Kessler, *Anza's 1779 Comanche Campaign* 13.
142   Kaelin, *American Indians of the Pikes Peak Region* 77.

Fe Trail and the explorations of Pike, Long, and Fremont. The westward expansion of the United States would have come to a standstill, perhaps for hundreds of years. Ute warriors, Ute scouts, Ute chiefs – the Ute Nation – were key players in this Turning Point of United States History.

Toad and Frog 143

Maqacaci (Horned Toad) lived with her family among the willows along a creek. One day her friend *Paqxwani* came for a visit.

"*Bakhe, Paqxwani, wuhgah!*"

Frog accepted her friend's invitation and slowly hopped into her house. She squatted by the door and examined the willow branches around and above them with a frown. She turned her thick neck toward the sound of the nearby water and pointed with her lips.

"You are going to drown," she calmly stated. "The water will take you."

Maqacaci said nothing but when Frog had left she thought to herself. *We better move.* She took all of her children and they found a new home high up on a hill. One morning as she lay warming herself in the sun *Paqxwani* returned.

"I am going to gather berries, would you like to come?"

Arm in arm, the old friends set off along the trail to the blackberry hill. *Paqxwani* talked without stopping, but Toad paid no attention.

"Heeeey. You don't listen to what I say. Why do I bother with you!" *Paqxwani* was angry with her friend. At this, *Maqacaci* filled her lungs with air and puffed herself up to twice her size.

"Old woman, you don't scare me! I'm going home." Frog croaked as she turned and left.

It began to rain, and it rained and rained. Frog

---

143   Smith, *Ute Tales* 24.

moved her home to a new pond on the top of the hill near Horned Toad.

"When the water goes away you are going to dry up and your feet will stick up in the air," *Maqacaci* warned her friend. But Frog was still angry, and looked the other way.

When Horned Toad returned a few days later there was Frog. On her back. All four feet in the air.

"Stupid old woman! I told you this would happen!" And with that she spit in her face.

"*Ahhhh*, that felt so good!" Frog yawned, and rubbed the moisture all over her parched skin. "I've been asleep, and I was so thirsty. Thank you my dear friend, thank you!"

WHAT CAN WE LEARN FROM "TOAD AND FROG?"

This legend always brings tears to my eyes as it was one that Loya and I frequently acted out together. One of the first times was during the Hayman Fire when I was scheduled to give a talk to the campers at Eleven Mile State Park. Loya and Kerry were visiting at our ranch and were only too willing to help me share the culture and stories of the Ute Nation.

It was in June, 2002, and the fire had been raging for several days, devouring over 110,000 acres. Just eleven miles south of the inferno, Eleven Mile State Park is situated in a broad mountain valley where its dam traps the frigid runoff of the South Platte River. The resulting reservoir is framed on all sides with jagged mountain ridges, spiked by blue-green pines and collared by wheat-colored grasses. On that day, wafting vapors of the thick heavy smoke snaked through the valley. Acrid smoke filled our nostrils as our audience fidgeted, glancing apprehensively at the glowing northern sky.

Loya and I looked at one another, and as grandmothers, knew what we had to do. Instead of the lecture we told of Toad and Frog.

Loya was a born actress and raconteur, her timing was perfect. First, she summarized the story in English and then switched to Ute. I jumped into the role of Frog as she became Toad. Arm in arm we acted out their convoluted friendship and everyone howled with laughter even though they didn't understand a word of Ute. Loya and I thoroughly enjoyed ourselves as I made my acting debut.

Powell had much to say about this type of storytelling among the Ute.

These fragmentary accounts are taught with great care and preserved with religious fidelity. Listening to such a relation one might suppose that the story was told for sport, but at another time he would discover that the most trivial act of the Indian's life was governed by the requirements of this traditional law, so that what at one moment appears to be a jest, at another is a solemn fact.

At night by the campfire the chief of the council or some venerable man [or woman] will tell one of these stories, and the elderly men of the band will enjoin especially upon the younger members to take heed of what is said. The chief relates the narrative and, whenever the circumstances are favorable, illustrates by acting a part, imitating the voice or actions of the several animal personages who are supposed to have taken part in the original scene, growling for the bear, chattering for the magpie, scolding for the Canada jay, chirping for the squirrel and hissing for the snake.

Often there is much dialogue when the elders take a part, and they will also assist in the acting. Sometimes a song is introduced in which, perhaps, the whole party will join. Perhaps while the principal actors are doing their parts, some person will interrupt them to comment on the wisdom or folly of such acts or to make some pertinent explanation for the benefit of the younger members of the tribe, and all seem much interested and greatly amused, bursting forth into loud laughter or screaming with wild delight.

There is usually a great deal of dialogue and much repetition and enumeration of many particulars...[144]

Later in July, as Loya and I Sun Danced together, this story helped to sustain me through the four challenging days of going without food and water, and dancing/praying in 120 degree heat. Our light cotton

144   Fowler, *Anthropology of the Numa* 73.

print dresses with open-flap, butterfly-winged sleeves somewhat helped catch any breeze. Our heads were crowned with a wreath of sage, as were our wrists and ankles. Days of unrelenting sun turned my face a beet red, while Loya's bronze skin never revealed its burn. My blue eyes watered and hurt, but her large brown eyes remained calm and serene. Wisps of my thin, brown hair tangled in my sage crown, while Loya's thick, silver braid remained elegant and impeccable all the way to her waist.

The third day, Saturday, is always the hardest. It is the longest day, with fewer rest periods between dance rounds because of all the special ceremonies at the Sacred Tree. The sun always seems the hottest then, and it feels as though Sunday, and completion, will never come. Late in the afternoon, as I prayed hard to complete my obligation, Toad popped into my head. I whispered to Loya through my cracked lips and cotton-filled mouth, "Can you please just spit on me?!"

Clifford, on the other hand, wasn't so easily amused – especially when I used Frog and Toad logic during one of our discussions. Unfortunately, I am quite opinionated and often stubborn. Our dialectic on one particular day had to do with the direction that my work should take. We were in Guatemala, on our way to ceremony with the World Council of Elders at Lake Antiqua. Clifford was clearly exasperated with me and I simply couldn't understand why he didn't agree with my "logical" viewpoint. He withdrew into a stony silence, his arms rigidly folded across his chest, staring out the bus window at the distant volcano. I was certain that he was re-evaluating his opinions in my favor. However, he turned abruptly, saying, "You know what? I'm going to give you a new name."

"Really? That's great! What will it be this time?"
"Tegupawat."
"Tegupawat? Cool. What does that mean?"

"She Who Talks Back. That's what it means: someone who always talks back. Not nice."

My feelings were hurt. I loved *Sunif Mamuch*, Wolf Woman, the name he had given me when he adopted me into the Ute Nation. But *Tegupawat*? Well, I was opinionated. I freely aired my viewpoint whether it was shared or not. Growing up with six brothers taught me that I had to stand up for myself. I guess *Tegupawat* was accurate, and it did fit me. I let out a deep sigh and turned to my teacher.

"Clifford, you're right. I am *Tegupawat*."

"No, no! That's a bad name! People don't like *Tegupawat*."

"But it is me! Thank you, Clifford. Thank you! I am *Tegupawat*."

Index of Ute Words

UTE	ENGLISH	PAGE
Sunif	Wolf	1-2, 9, 14, 107, 109-110, 115-117, 121, 123-126, 129-130, 135-137, 143-145, 199
Tamau'errawats	Morning	41
Tapai Mawisika	East	91
Tau-shants	Antelope	23-24, 135
Tavooch, also Tav-weatch, or Tov-wots, or Tavooch	First Rabbit	33-34, 86-87
To-go-av, also Togoa	Rattlesnake	21, 24, 50-51
To-go-i	Cache in the rocks or cave	111-114
Tonapagari	Lightning	42
Tov-wots, also Tav-weatch	Coyote's father	33, 126, 135
Tso-a-vwits, also Unupits	Witch	45, 48-52
Tu-gwe-nai	Stories, Legends	11, 38
Tu-gwe-wa-gunt	Storyteller	10-11, 13, 38
Tum-pwi-nai-ro-gwi-nump	Stone Shirt	17, 26, 135
Tununiri	Thunder	42, 64-65
Turasanagovi	Gum Weed	69
Tu-wap	Piñon Pine	121
Uja	Sage Grouse	48-49
U-rai-go-i	Cache in the ground	111-114
Us, also Wiisi	Yucca	121
Ututatapi	Autumn, Fall	45
W'ni thokunup	Morache	67-68
Yahowitz	Coyote	91, 107, 109-110, 115, 121, 123-125, 129-130, 135-136, 143
Yu-a-nump	Rabbit Bush	36

Bibliography

Bray, Warwick. *Everyday Life of the Aztecs*. Dorset Press, 1968.

Carson, Phil. *Across the Northern Frontier: Spanish Explorations in Colorado*. Johnson Books, 1998.

Cassels, E. Steve. *The Archaeology of Colorado*. Johnson Publishing, 1990.

Castaneda, Pedro Reyes. *The Journey of Coronado: 1540-1542*. http://www.pbs.org/weta/thewest/resources/archives/one/corona2.htm, Accessed 20 Nov 2014.

Chavez, Fray Angelico, translator, and Ted J. Warner, ed. *The Dominguez-Escalante Journal: Their Expedition Through Colorado, Utah, Arizona, and New Mexico in 1776*. Utah UP, 1995.

Cushing, Frank Hamilton. *My Adventures in Zuni*. Filter Press, 1998.

Densmore, Frances. *Northern Ute Music*. Washington, D.C.: Government Printing Office, 1922.

Emmitt, Robert. *The Last War Trail: The Utes and the Settlement of Colorado*. University of Oklahoma Press, 1954.

--. "Indians in Colorado." *The Denver Westerner's Brand Book*. Ed. L. Coulson Hageman. Vol. XXX-XXXI. Denver: Westerners, 1977. 319. Print.

Fowler, Catherine S. and Don D. *Anthropology of the Numa: John Wesley Powell's Manuscripts on the Numic Peoples of Western North America, 1868-1880*. Smithsonian Institution Press, 1971.

Gilbert, Adrian G. and Maurice M. Cotterell. *The Mayan Prophecies*. Barnes & Noble Books, 1995.

Holmer, Rick. *The Aztec Book of Destiny*. BookSurge, 2005.

Hutchinson, Art and Jack E. Smith, editors. *Proceedings of the Anasazi Symposium 1991*. Mesa Verde Museum Association, Inc. 1991.

James, Susan E. "Some Aspects of the Aztec Religion in the Hopi Kachina Cult." *Journal of the Southwest*, vol. 42, no. 4, 2000, p. 897.

--. "Mimetic Rituals of Child Sacrifice in the Hopi Kachina Cult." *Journal of the Southwest*, vol. 44, no. 3, 2002, 337-356.

Jenkins, John Major. *Maya Cosmogenesis 2012*. Bear & Company, 1998.

John, Elizabeth A.H. *Storms Brewed in Other Men's Worlds*. Oklahoma UP, 1996.

Kantner, John. *Ancient Puebloan Southwest*. Cambridge UP, 2004

Kaelin, Celinda Reynolds. *American Indians of the Pikes Peak Region*. Arcadia Publishing, 2008.

Kaelin, Celinda Reynolds. *Pikes Peak Backcountry*. Caxton Press, 1999.

Kessler, Ronald E. *Anza's 1779 Comanche Campaign*. 2nd ed., Adobe Village Press, 2001.

Kimmett, Leo. *Florissant, Colorado.* Rev. ed, Master Printers, 1980.

Kohl, Michael F. and John S. McIntosh, editor. *Discovering Dinosaurs in the Old West – The Field Journals of Arthur Lakes.* Smithsonian Institution Press, 1997.

LeBlanc, Steven A. *Prehistoric Warfare in the American Southwest.* Utah UP, 1999.

Lekson, Stephen H. *A History of the Ancient Southwest.* School for Advanced Research Press, 2008.

Leon-Portilla, Miguel. *Fifteen Poets of the Aztec World.* Oklahoma UP, 1992.

-- (). *Aztec Thought and Culture.* Translated by Jack Emory Davis, Oklahoma UP, 1963.

Lister, Florence C. *In the Shadow of the Rocks: Archaeology of the Chimney Rock District in Southern Colorado.* The Herald Press, 1997.

Lister, Robert H. and Florence C. Lister. *Chaco Canyon: Archaeology & Archaeologists.* New Mexico UP, 1981.

Madsen, David B. and David Rhode, editors. *Across the West: Human Population Movement and the Expansion of the Numa.* Utah UP, 1994.

Martinez, Wilfred O. *Anza and Cuerno Verde: Decisive Battle.* El Escritorio, 2001.

Miller, Mary and Karl Taube. *The Gods and Symbols of Ancient Mexico and the Maya.* Thames and Hudson Ltd., 1993.

Mendosa, Patrick M. *Song of Sorrow: Massacre at Sand Creek.* Willow Wind Publishing, 1993.

Muench, David and Donald G. Pike. *Anasazi: Ancient People of the Rock.* American West Publishing Co., 1974.

Nicholson, H.B. *Topiltzin Quetzalcoatl: The Once and Future Lord of the Toltecs.* Colorado UP, 2001.

Prucha, Francis Paul. *The Great Father: The United States Government and the American Indians.* Nebraska UP, 1986.

Recinos, Adrian, translator. *Popol Vuh.* English version by Delia Goeta and Sylvanus G.Morley. Oklahoma UP, 1950.

Reed, Paul F., editor. *Chaco's Northern Prodigies: Salmon, Aztec, and the Ascendancy of the Middle San Juan Region after AD 1100.* Utah UP, 2008.

--. *The Puebloan Society of Chaco Canyon.* Greenwood Press, 2004.

Robinson, Charles M. *Bad Hand: A Biography of General Ranald S. MacKenzie.* State House Press, 1993.

Sagstetter, Beth and Bill. *The Cliff Dwellings Speak.* Benchmark Publishing of Colorado, 2010.

Schele, Linda and Peter Mathews. *The Code of Kings: The Language of Seven Sacred Maya Temples and Tombs.* Touchstone by Simon & Schuster, 1998.

Simmons, Virginia M. *The Ute Indians of Utah, Colorado, and New Mexico.* Colorado UP, 2000.

Smith, Anne M. *Ethnography of the Northern Utes.* Museum of New Mexico Press, 1974.

--. *Ute Tales.* Utah UP, 1992.

Stuart, David E. *Anasazi America*. New Mexico UP, 2000.

Swanton, John R. *The Indian Tribes of North America*. Smithsonian Institution Press, 1969.

Turner, Christy G. and Jacqueline A. Turner. *Man Corn: Cannibalism and Violence in the Prehistoric American Southwest*. Utah UP, 1999.

Unitah-Ouray Ute Tribe. *Stories of Our Ancestors: A Collection of Northern-Ute Indian Tales*. Utah UP, 1974.

Ute Dictionary. Ute Press of the Southern Ute Tribe, 1979.

Waldman, Carl. *Atlas of the North American Indian*. Facts On File, Inc., 1985.

Warner, Ted J., editor and Fray Angelico Chavez, translator. *The Dominguez-Escalante Journal*. Utah UP, 1995.

Waters, Frank, and Oswals White Bear Fredericks. *The Book of the Hopi*. Viking Penguin Books, 1963.

BIBLIOGRAPHY, ARTICLES

Foerster, Brien, Mysterious Toltec Civilization of Mexico.
   Retrieved from (http://hiddenincatours.com)

Klotz, Irene. (2012, March 14) *New Clovis Comet Clues from
   Mexico.* Retrieved from (http://News.Discovery.Com/
   Irene-Klotz.Htm)

Stanley, Steven M., Ed., (University of Hawaii, Honolulu, HI,
   and approved January 31, 2012) Elsabel Israde-
   Alcantaraa, et.al. (2012) *Evidence from Central Mexico
   Supporting the Younger Dryas Extraterrestrial Impact
   Hypothesis.* Retrieved from (http://www.pnas.org/
   content/early/2012/03/01/1110614109.abstract).

Williams, Jack S. (2001) "Making sense of the leather jacket
   (Cueras) worn in Northern New Spain." *San Diego
   History Journal,* 73 *(Winter)* The Center for Spanish
   Colonial Research. San Diego, CA., 44-63.

United States Secretary of the Interior, Henry M. Teller. *Annual
   Report for American Indian Religious Crimes,* 01 Nov
   1883.

Roberts, John. (2003, July/August). Riddles of the Anasazi.
   Smithsonian Magazine. Retrieved from (http://www.
   smithsonianmag.com/history)

"Clovis Comet & North American Mass Extinction." *www.
   SciForums.com.* http://www.sciforums.com/threads/
   clovis-comet-north-american-mass-extinction.81801/.
   02 Jan 2009.

AUTHOR INTERVIEWS

Duncan, Clifford. Personal interview. 10 Mar 1998.

Duncan, Clifford. Personal interview. 22 Apr 1998.

Duncan, Clifford. Personal interview. 07 May 1998.

Duncan, Clifford. Personal interview. 05 Aug 2000.

Duncan, Clifford. Personal interview. 11 Sept 2003.

Duncan, Clifford. Interviews by author, Florissant, CO: 3/10/98; 4/22/98; 5/7/98.

Duncan, Clifford. Interviews by author, Central and South America, various locations, 8/5/2000 to 9/11/2003.

Duncan, Clifford. Various workshops and Elderhostel classes, 1995 to 2000.

Arrum, Loya. Ongoing friendship, work together, and fellow Sun Dancers from 2000 to 2013. Adopted Ute sister.

Cesspooch, Kerry. Ongoing friendship, work together, and fellow Sun Dancers from 2000 to 2013. Adopted Ute sister.

Barrios, Mercedes. Mayan Priest, journeys with Clifford and visits at the ranch, 2000 to 2003.

Illustrations

BY MANUEL PULIDO

CPSIA information can be obtained
at www.ICGtesting.com
Printed in the USA
FFOW05n2132260417